Woman Poet

YO-BRF-785

Woman Poet

WOMEN-IN-LITERATURE, INCORPORATED

Reno 1981

WOMEN-IN-LITERATURE, INCORPORATED

P.O. Box 12668, Reno, Nevada 89510

Cover photo of Audre Lorde by Lynda Koolish

Acknowledgments: An earlier version of Part 1 of Yvonne's "The Tearing of the Skin" appeared in *Willmore City* in 1977; the complete poem was copyrighted in 1979 by Yvonne. Robin Morgan's poems "Documentary" and "Lunch Hour" were copyrighted in 1981 by Robin Morgan. Akua Lezli Hope's poems "No One Comes Home to Lonely Women" and "To Sister for Mother" were copyrighted in 1980 by Akua Lezli Hope. Adrienne Rich's complete interview of Lorde was initiated in full by Women-in-Literature, Inc., for *Woman Poet*. As a special courtesy, we have given over the copyright to *Signs*, of the University of Chicago Press, and they copyrighted it in 1981. Yet, for that section of the interview herein printed, we retain present and future limited rights—for any use specifically by *Woman Poet* and/or Women-in-Literature, Inc.

Due to a delay in our publication date, some of the material in this anthology has been previously published; we have given the permissions needed for this.

Library of Congress Catalog Card Number: 81-69793
International Standard Book Number: 0-935634-02-9 (paper)
0-935634-03-7 (hardcover)
International Standard Serial Number: 0195-6183

Manufactured in the United States of America

FIRST EDITION

This publication was helped by grants from the National Endowment for the Arts through the Nevada State Council on the Arts and from the American Association of University Women. We thank them for their support.

Woman Poet

Editor-in-Chief — Elaine Dallman
Guest Editor — Marilyn Hacker
Poetry Editor — Carolyn Kizer
Special Editorial Advisors — Barbara Mello
Laurel Ross
Catharine Stimpson
Shirley Owen Taft
Editorial Board — Joyce Cohen
Jessica Devin
Elizabeth Francis
Marsha Gasperoni
Janne Hanrahan
Dorothy Kline
Adrianne Marcus
Pamela Pavlovsky
Nancy Pulver
Earline Mason Reid
Layle Silbert
Shirley Sousa
Editorial Assistants — Virginia Kristensen
Barbara K. Powderly
Marketing/Distribution — Adela Bishop
Marcia Freedman (Israel)
Charlene Eley
JoAn Johnstone
Susanne Müller
(Switzerland)
Frances Walker
Woman unLtd (United
Kingdom)

Editorial Correspondence
Elaine Dallman, Woman Poet,
P.O. Box 12668, Reno, Nevada 89510

Submissions
Virginia Kristensen, Editorial Assistant,
P.O. Box 35, Los Gatos, California 95030.

We welcome unsolicited submissions by writers. Work must be original and unpublished in any version. We reserve the right to reprint. Work which would appear simultaneously in our anthology and an author's collection will be considered if crediting of *Woman Poet* is possible.

We wish we could read all manuscripts in one day's turnaround. We apologize that we cannot. Please allow a minimum of eight weeks for our volunteer editorial staff to carefully read your manuscript. Delays imply no disrespect for the work submitted but reflect the limitations imposed by too heavy a workload.

If work is to be returned, it must be accompanied by a self-addressed envelope with sufficient postage.

Publisher
Women-in-Literature, Incorporated, a non-profit publisher, P.O. Box 12668, Reno, Nevada 89510.

Subscriptions
Charter subscriptions or 4 volume sets beginning with any designated volume, U.S.A.: institutions $28.00, individuals $20.00, students $18.00. Other countries add $3.00 to cover postage.

Classroom Discount Rates
Please write for special classroom discount rates. Free teacher's subscription with classroom adoption.

Payment
Nevada residents add 5¾% sales tax.

Checks should be payable to *Woman Poet*, P.O. Box 12668, Reno, Nevada 89510.

Advertising Rates
Correspondence about advertising inserts should be addressed to *Woman Poet*, Department A, P.O. Box 12668, Reno, Nevada 89510.

Change of Address
Please notify the press and local postmaster immediately, providing *both* the old and the new address. *Allow 6 weeks for change.* Claims for missing volumes should be made within one month of publication. The publishers will supply missing volumes free only when losses have been sustained in transit and reserve stock will permit.

Woman Poet

VOLUME II

The East

Staff Note   10
Preface   11

AUDRE LORDE
  October   13
  The Evening News   13
  Morning Is a Time for Miracles   14

Critical Response

Full Stature: Audre Lorde   15
  Joan Larkin

Interview with Audre Lorde   18
  Adrienne Rich

Biographical Notes   22

Judith Johnson Sherwin
  Miranda's Birthspell   23

Robin Morgan
  Documentary   26
  Lunch Hour   28

Jane Miller
  Lightning Storm   29
  6 a.m.   30
  5 a.m.   30
  The Long Fingers of 1956   31

Colette Inez
  Reading da Leaves   32

Carol Muske
  Chapter One   33
  Special Delivery to Curtis: The Future
    of the World   34

Sonya Dorman
  Two Poets on the Way to the Palace   35
  Whodunit   35

Judith Moffett
  "Cambridge University Swimming
    Club / No Public Access to River"   36

MARIE PONSOT
  Half-Life: Copies to All Concerned   40
  "Sois Sage O Ma Douleur"   40
  Late   43
  On the Country Sleep of
    Susanne K. Langer   44

Critical Response

Queens' Secrets: The Poems
  of Marie Ponsot   45
  Cynthia Macdonald

Interview with Marie Ponsot   48
  Rosemary Deen

Biographical Notes   51

Celia Gilbert
  The Stone Maiden   53
  At the Ball   53

Joan Larkin
Sleeping on the Left Side   54
Cow's Skull with Calico Roses   54

Cynthia Macdonald
The Mosaic Hunchback   56
Remains—Stratigraphy   58

Toi Derricotte
The Testimony of Sister Maureen   59

Yvonne
The Tearing of the Skin   62

Kinereth Gensler
The Border   67

Marge Piercy
Shadows of the Burning   69
Night Fight   70

Jane Augustine
After Yeats   71
I Help My Mother Move Out
of Her Old House in the Country   71

Kathleen Spivack
Humanitarian   73

Ntozake Shange
jonestown or the disco   74

Lois Elaine Griffith
For All the Homesick Sunshine Girls
in Spring   76
Fire Wind's Song to Sundae (Loba)   77

Celia Watson Strome
Nr. 6   78
Nr. 10   78
Nr. 12   79
Nr. 19   79

Phyllis Janowitz
Mrs. Lucky   80

Judith McDaniel
When Mother Died, Rows of Cans   81
Snow in April   81

JUNE JORDAN
This Is a Poem about Vieques,
Puerto Rico   83
Poem about a Night Out: Michael:
Good-Bye for Awhile   84
Poem for Inaugural Rose   85
Poem Nr. 2 for Inaugural Rose   85

Critical Response
This Wheel's on Fire: The Poetry of
June Jordan   87
Sara Miles
Interview with June Jordan   90
Karla M. Hammond
Biographical Notes   94

Kristina McGrath
Sequence from Blue to Blue   97

Sharon Olds
Homage   99
The Mole   99

Ellen Wittlinger
Waiting   100
In Cahoots   100
Someone You Love   101
Red   101

Akua Lezli Hope
No One Comes Home
to Lonely Women   102
To Sister for Mother   103

Ann Lauterbach
The Yellow Linen Dress: A Sequence   104

Barbara Howes
Shunpike   106
A Point of View   106

Irena Klepfisz
Contexts   107

Kathleen Lignell
To Say Whose Side You're on   109

Sara Miles
Native Dancer   110
More   111
Talking about It   111

Honor Moore
Poem: For the Beginning   113
Abundance and Scarcity   114

Barbara Guest
Quilts   116

Marilyn Hacker
Feeling and Form   119

Contributors' Notes   121

Staff Note

Lynda Koolish

Marilyn Hacker (Guest Editor) wrote *Presentation Piece* (Viking), which received the National Book Award in Poetry for 1975. She also wrote *Separations* and *Taking Notice* (both by Knopf, 1976 & 1980). She is an editor of *The Little Magazine*. In 1980 she received a Guggenheim Fellowship as well as a New York Creative Artists Public Service grant. She and her daughter, Iva, live in Manhattan.

Preface

BY THE EDITORS

An anthology is a kind of community, and WOMAN POET is one to which we are proud to belong. A series of anthologies is a community in a state of flux and growth, a dialogue between writer and writer, and writer and reader. If you, readers and writers, find us useful, you can play a part in making sure that the next issue involving your region makes up for any omissions you find in this volume. We need to be in touch with Hispanic and Asian-American writers in particular; we need to be in touch with small states with relatively large populations, like Rhode Island and Delaware, and with large states with small populations, like the Dakotas. We depend on you, our readers and writers, to help us to make WOMAN POET truly representative of American women in all our superb variety and growing strength. And please remember that WOMAN POET is not a magazine. It is a regional anthology, a book in fact, and subject to the delays which in book publishing seem inevitable. Be patient with us. Your support, both moral and financial, will make us more efficient. WOMAN POET, in this sense, is really representative of American women today, because we are learning as we go, with the gathering confidence which our skills give to us— our skills, and your praise.

DEDICATION

We dedicate this issue to the memory
of Muriel Rukeyser (1913–1980),
her heroism, her beauty, her courage,
in her art and in her life.

Audre Lorde

STATEN ISLAND, NEW YORK

Anna Kaufman Moon

October

Spirits of the abnormally born
live on in water
and the heroically dead
in the entrails of snake
I span my days now like a wild bridge
swaying in place
caught between poems like a vise
I am finishing my piece of this bargain
and how shall I return?

Seboulisa mother of power
keeper of birds, fat and beautiful
give me the strength in your eyes

to remember
what I have learned
help me to attend with passion
these tasks at my hand for doing:

Carry me to some shore
that my feet will not shatter
do not let me pass away
before I have a name
for this tree under which I am lying
do not let me die
still
needing to be stranger.

1978

The Evening News

    First rule of the road
    attend quiet victims first.

I am kneading my bread Winnie Mandela
and children who sing in the streets of Soweto
are jailed for inciting to riot
the moon in Soweto is mad
is bleeding my sister into the earth
is mixing her seed with the vultures'
Greeks reap her like olives out of the trees
she is skimmed like salt
from the skin of a hungry desert
while the Ganvié fisherwomen   with milk-large breasts
hide a fish with the face of a small girl
in the prow of their boats.

Winnie Mandela I am feeling your face
with the pain of my crippled fingers
our children   are escaping
their birth in the streets
of Soweto and Brooklyn
what does it mean
our wars
being fought by our children?

Winnie Mandela our names are like olives, salt, sand
opal, amber, obsidian
that hide their shapes well.
We have never touched shaven foreheads together
yet how many of our sisters' and daughters' bones

whiten in secret
whose names we have not yet spoken
whose names we have never spoken
I have never heard their names
spoken.

Second rule of the road
any wound will stop bleeding
if you press down hard enough.

Morning Is a Time for Miracles

(to B. G.)

A core of the conversations we never had
lies in the distance
between your need and mine
a piece of each
buried beneath the wall which separates
our sameness
a talisman of birth
hidden at the root of your mother's spirit
my mother's fury.

Now reaching for you with my sad words
between sleeping and waking
a runic stone speaks
what is asked for is destroyed
by the words that must seek it
like dew in the early morning dissolving
the tongue of salt as well as its thirst
and I call you secret names of praise and fire
that sound like your birthright but are not
the names of friend
while you hide from me under 100 excuses
lying like tombstones along the road
between your house and mine.

I could accept a blame I understood
but picking over the fresh and possible lonelinesses
of this too-early morning
I find the relics of my history
fossilized into a prison
where I learn to make love forever
better than how to make friends
where you are encased like a halfstoned peach
in the rigid art of your healing
and in case you have ever tried to reach me
and I couldn't hear you

these words are in place of the dead air
still between us:

A memorial to the conversations we won't be
        having
to laughter shared and important
as the selves we helped make real
but also to the dead
revelations we buried stillborn
in the refuse of fear and silence
and your remembered eyes
which don't meet mine anymore.

I never intended to let you slip through my fingers
nor to ever purchase your interest
like the desire of a whore
who yawns behind her upturned hand
pretending a sigh of pleasure
I have had that, too, already.

Once I thought when I opened my eyes we would
        move
into a freer and more open country
where the sun could illuminate our different desires
and the fresh air do us honor for who we were
yet I have awakened at 4 A.M. with a ribald joke to
        tell you
and found I had lost the name of the street
where you hid under an assumed name
and I knew I would have to bleed again
in order to find you,
but just once
in the possibilities of this too-early morning
I wanted you
to talk
not as a healer
but as a lonely woman
talking to a friend.

1978

Full Stature: Audre Lorde

BY JOAN LARKIN

I FIRST HEARD AUDRE LORDE'S voice on tape on Mother's Day, 1972, as I was listening to a public radio broadcast of women poets. An amused, melodic voice drew me bodily, telling me to stir myself. The poet, to me then unknown, was speaking in clear, subtle lyrics about pregnancy, birth, and the separateness of a daughter growing in her own way:

> I thought
> Now her hands
> Are formed, and her hair
> Has started to curl
> Now her teeth are done
> Now she sneezes.
> Then the seed opened.
> I bore you one morning just before spring—
> My head rang like a fiery piston
> My legs were towers between which
> A new world was passing.
> (Now That I Am Forever with Child)

In these early poems from *The First Cities* (Poets' Press, 1968) are threads that have developed through Lorde's later books to the most recent, seemingly different, and astonishingly powerful work.

In Lorde's second book, *Cables to Rage* (Paul Breman, London, 1970), the subjects of blood connection, necessary separation, and selfhood are resonant with dangers of a world beyond the personal:

> Shall I split
> or be cut down
> by a word's complexion or the lack of it
> and from what direction
> will the opening be made
> to show the true face of me
> lying exposed and together

> my children your children their children
> bent on our conjugating business.
> (Bloodbirth)

By the third book, *From a Land Where Other People Live* (Broadside, 1973), the contradictions of mothering have become both dominant subject and metaphor. Both this and *New York Head Shop and Museum* (Broadside, 1974) contain several poems directly addressed to Lorde's children, her own mother, other women and their children. But the emphasis in the poet's voice is different. It is now explicitly concerned with power—woman, Black, human. Its context has moved from the generalized (and literary) landscape of earth, seasons, and time to our specific location in history. Lorde tells of the violence, the terrible everyday pain, of individual lives, and of tragedies documented in headlines: Malcolm, Birmingham, fruitless peace marches.

The images are urban: phone booths, graffiti, supermarkets, luncheonettes, tv's, toilets "made of glass/wired for sound." The environment is filled with the junk and shit—verbal and physical—that destroy our power and seduce and drug our children:

> Even though all astronauts are white
> Perhaps Black People *can* develop
> Some of those human attributes
> Requiring
> Dried dog food frozen coffee instant oatmeal
> Depilatories deodorants detergents
> And other assorted plastic.

Even the titles of the poems are plainspoken, full of sardonic humor, as in the excerpt quoted above from "The American Cancer Society or There Is More than One Way to Skin a Coon," and in "The

Brown Menace or Poem to the Survival of Roaches."
There is no trusty rhetoric, no easy sentimental-
ity. She speaks unpleasing truths with militant
assurance.

The early theme of a mother's lessons that will be
transformed or forgotten by her children has now
developed into Lorde's acceptance of her own au-
thority as poet, mythmaker, messenger. The role fills
her with dread:

> I am afraid of speaking
> the truth
> in a room on the 17th floor
> my body is dreaming
> it sits
> bottom pinned to a table
> eating perpetual watermelon inside my own
>   head.

However, she knows that her students are waiting

> for what I am sworn to tell them
> for what they least want to hear.
>   (Blackstudies)

From a Land Where Other People Live was nomi-
nated for a National Book Award for 1973, and
Coal, which included poems from previous small-
press books, was published in a handsome hard-
cover edition by W. W. Norton in 1976. Perhaps
these indicate a widening audience. Certainly they
show a deserved, overdue recognition from the
(white, male) literary establishment. But these val-
idations were never the sources of that fire Lorde
keeps striking—*for us*, I want to say—since now,
with greater urgency than in that early radio broad-
cast, Lorde is not merely speaking, but *speaking to*.

The seven long poems of *Between Our Selves*,
beautifully printed in a limited edition by a small
press (Eidolon Editions, 1976), the recording *A
Sign/I Was Not Alone* (Out & Out Books, 1977),
talks, public readings, and women's writing work-
shops across the United States and at international
conferences in Russia and Africa—all vibrate with
Lorde's consciousness of a living audience. The bur-
geoning community of women hearers and writers
energizes, grounds, and demands growth. For Lorde
it seems to have permitted the full development of a
particular oracular, prophetic quality. In *The Black
Unicorn* (W. W. Norton, 1978), Lorde's most recent

and longest book (it includes all the poems pub-
lished in *Between Our Selves* and recorded in *A
Sign/I Was Not Alone*, as well as 56 others), the
world is here, the other person is here, more audible
than before:

> Her poem reached like an arc across country
>   and
> "I'm trying to hear you" I said
> roaring with my pain in a predawn city
> where it is open season on black children
> where my worst lullaby goes on over and over.
>   (The Same Death Over and Over)

In such poems, which racist violence and murder oc-
casion, Lorde echoes earlier knowledge, but reaches
beyond in wisdom and mastery. She has learned that
a source of hate is dread of those parts of ourselves
we refuse to acknowledge and integrate:

> who do you think me to be
> that you are terrifed of becoming
> or what do you see in my face
> you have not already discarded
> in your own mirror.
>   (Outside)

In a poem of libation and prayer to Seboulisa, the
Abomey mother goddess, Lorde dedicates herself to
the task of speech and prays

> give me the woman strength
> of tongue in this cold season.
>   (125th Street and Abomey)

She can frequently expose a deep vein of irony,
while still affirming her work as a teller of unre-
garded truth.

> My words are blind children I have armed
> . . . .
> I am scarred and marketed
> like a streetcorner in Harlem
> a woman
> whose face in the tiles
> your feet have not yet regarded
> . . . .
> the woman you cannot deal with
> I am the mouth
> of your scorn.
>   (A Small Slaughter)

Personal growth is a long labor. In "Power," one of the most important poems of our time, the shooting of Clifford Glover, a ten-year-old black child, by a white cop, and the subsequent co-opting of the one black woman member by the acquitting jury, provoke grief, rage, and the cutting edge of analysis. However, Lorde also examines her own potential for corruption, and for all despisals fueled by rhetoric. She demonstrates the agonizing self-dialogue needed "to touch the destruction within me: "lest

> my power too will run corrupt as poisonous mold
> or lie limp and useless as an unconnected wire.

To name the self authentically, she incorporates, deeply, the legends, rituals, and traditions of Dahomey (whose Amazons were prized women warriors) and of the Yoruba peoples of western Nigeria. I cannot claim familiarity with the pantheon of the Orisha, but Lorde knows and lives with it. She invokes the goddess of Abomey as mother:

> Head bent, walking through snow
> I see you Seboulisa
> printed inside the back of my head

Though

> Half earth and time splits us apart
> like struck rock.
>   (125th Street and Abomey)

she finds a fruitful self in this ancient matrilineal connection. Her self-creation is erotic, female, as well as spiritual, deeply rooted in the body as a source of energy and love. This creation also appears in her recent prose (see especially *Uses of the Erotic*). For both prose and poetry, other women often participate with her. The mature power of Lorde's love poems affirm this process. They are rich, sensuous, sure of what they know:

> women exchanging blood
> in the innermost rooms of moment
> we must taste of each other's fruit
> at least once
> before we shall both be slain.
>   (Meet)

In attempting to elucidate Lorde's vision, I have scarcely spoken of her craft, her fearless use of prosaic declarations, her surprising images. The musical sounds in "Dahomey": "Eshu's iron quiver," "erect and flamingly familiar," and "mute as a porcupine in a forest of lead" are contrasts. This music flows in tension with frequent severity of statement:

> Bearing two drums on my head I speak
> whatever language is needed
> to sharpen the knives of my tongue.

After the delight of hearing Audre Lorde read aloud, it comes as a blessing to find these contrasts easily determinable on the page: for example in "Chain," a poem based on a news item about two girls impregnated by their father, not rhetoric, but the primal intensity of simple statements in the girls' imagined voices creates the effect of nightmare, of inescapable meanings. In *The Black Unicorn*, her most powerful and important book to date, I see a woman's mind grown to full stature, and a voice whose capacities have increased with exercise: musicality; self-assurance; the breath-conditioned phrasing of a language meant to be spoken aloud; the wide range through which she travels (sometimes in shocking, swift turn-about) from crooning lullaby to fiery condemnation, or from passionate intimacy or meditative self-dialogue to haunting litany and healing public speech.

Layle Silbert

JOAN LARKIN is a founding editor of Out & Out Books, which published the LP record *A Sign/ I Was Not Alone*. She has read her work from coast to coast and produced several radio programs in a series, "The Poet's Craft." A CAPS winner in 1976 and in 1979, she teaches writing at Brooklyn College. *Housework* (1975), her original poems, was published by Out & Out Books.

Interview with Audre Lorde

BY ADRIENNE RICH

Question: What do you mean when you say that those two essays—"Poems Are Not Luxuries"[1] and "Uses of the Erotic"[2]—are really progressions?

AL: They're part of something that's not finished yet. I don't know what the rest of it is, but they're very clear progressions to me, in feeling out something that is connected also with the first piece of prose I ever wrote. The one thread I feel coming through over and over in my life is the battle to preserve my perceptions, the battle to win through and to keep them—pleasant or unpleasant, painful or whatever—

Question: And however much they were denied.

AL: And however much they were denied. And however painful some of them were. When I think of the way in which I courted punishment, the way in which I just swam into it: "If this is the only way you're going to deal with me, you're gonna have to deal with me this way."

Question: You're talking about as a young child?

AL: I'm talking about as an infant, as a very very young child. And then over and over again throughout my life. I kept myself through feeling. I lived through it. And at such a subterranean level, I think, that I didn't know *how* to talk. I was really busy feeling out other ways of getting and giving information and whatever else if I could, because talking wasn't where it was at.

People were talking all around me all the time— and not either getting or giving much that was useful to them or to me, or that made sense to me at the time.

Question: And not listening to what you tried to say, if you did speak.

AL: When you asked how I began writing, I told you how poetry functioned specifically for me from the time I was very young, from nursery rhymes. When someone said to me, "How do you feel?" or "What do you think?" or asked another direct question, I would recite a poem, and somewhere in that poem would be the feeling, somewhere in it would be the piece of information. It might be a line. It might be an image. The poem was my response.

Question: Like a translation into this poem which already existed, of something you knew in a pre-verbal way. So the poem became your language?

AL: Yes. I remember reading in the children's room of the library, I couldn't have been past the second or third grade, but I remember the book. It was illustrated by Arthur Rackham, a book of poems. These were old books; the library in Harlem used to get the oldest books, in the worst condition. Walter de la Mare's "The Traveller"—I will never forget that poem.

Question: Where the traveller rides up to the door of the empty house?

AL: That's right. He knocks at the door and nobody answers. "'Is there anybody there?' he said." That poem imprinted itself on me. And finally, he's beating down the door and nobody answers, and

[1] "Poems Are Not Luxuries," *Chrysalis* Nr. 3, 1977.
[2] "Uses of the Erotic," Out & Out Books Pamphlet Nr. 3, 1978.
*For other portions of Rich's interview, see *Signs: Journal of Women in Culture and Society*, VI, Nr. 4.

he has a feeling that there really is somebody in there. And then he turns his horse and he says, "'Tell them I came, and nobody answered. That I kept my word,' he said." I used to recite that poem to myself all the time. It was one of my favorites. And if you'd asked me what is it about, I don't think I could have told you. But this was the first cause of my own writing, my need to say things I couldn't say otherwise, when I couldn't find other poems to serve.

Question: You had to make your own.

AL: There were so many complex emotions, it seemed, for which poems did not exist, I had to find a secret way to express my feelings. I used to memorize my poems. I would say them out, I didn't write them down. I had this long fund of poetry in my head. I remember trying when I was in high school not to think in poems. I saw the way other people thought, and it was an amazement to me—step by step, not in bubbles up from chaos that you had to anchor with words. When I wrote something that finally had it, I would say it aloud and it would start to sift in, keep coming to me. It would start repeating itself and I'd know, that's struck, that's true. Like a bell. Something struck true. And there the words would be.

*

Question: You were ill when you were called to go down to Tougaloo?

AL: Yes, I felt—I had almost died.

Question: What was going on?

AL: Diane di Prima—that was 1967—had started the Poets' Press; and she said, "You know, it's time you had a book." And I said, "Well, who's going to print it?" I was going to put those poems away, because I had found I was revising too much instead of writing new poems, and that's how I found out, again through experience, that poetry is not play dough. You can't take a poem and keep re-forming it. It is itself, and you have to know how to cut it, and if there's something else you want to say, that's fine. But I was repolishing and repolishing, and Diane said, "You have to print these. Put 'em out." And the Poets' Press published *The First Cities*. Well, I worked on that

book, getting it together, and it was going into press. I had gotten the proofs back and I started repolishing again and realized, "This is going to be a book!" Putting myself on the line. People I don't even know are going to read these poems. What's going to happen? It felt very critical, and I was in an absolute blaze of activity because things financially were so bad at home. And I went out and got a job. I was with the two kids in the daytime and worked at the library at night. Jonathan used to cry every night when I left and I would hear his shrieks going down this long hall to the elevator. I was working nights, and I'd apprenticed myself to a stained glass windowmaker, and I was working in my mother's office, and making Christmas for my friends, and I became very ill—I had overdone it. I was too sick to get up, and Ed answered the phone. It was Galen Williams from the Poetry Center asking if I'd like to go as poet in residence to Tougaloo, a Black college in Mississippi. I'd been recommended for a grant. It was Ed who said, "You have to do this." My energy was at such a low ebb that I couldn't see how—first of all, it was very frightening to me, the idea of someone responding to me as a poet. This book, by the way, hadn't even come out yet, you understand?

Question: And suddenly you were already being taken seriously by unseen people out there.

AL: That's right. In particular, I was asked to be public; to speak *as*, rather than *to*. But I felt as if I'd come back from the dead at that point, and so everything was up for grabs. I thought, "hey, very good, let's see"—not because I felt I could do it; I just knew it was new and different. I was terrified to go South. Then there were echoes of an old dream: I had wanted to go to Tougaloo years before. My friend Elaine and I were going to join the Freedom Riders in Jackson when we left California in 1961 to return to New York, and Elaine's mother got down on her knees in San Francisco and begged us please not to do this, that they would kill us, and we didn't do it. So going to Tougaloo in Jackson was part of the mythic—

Question: But it sounds as if, before, you had been

more romantic about what going South would mean, and six years later, with two kids *and* everything that happened in between in the South—

AL: I was scared. I thought: "I'm going." Really, it was the first thing that countered the fury and pain I felt at leaving that little boy screaming every night. It was like—all right, if I can walk out and hear that child screaming in order to go down to the library and work every night, then I'm gonna be able at least to do something that I want to find out about. So I went. The ways in which I was on the line in Tougaloo . . . . I began to learn about courage, I began to learn to talk. But this was a small group and there was a dynamic between us. We became very close. I learned so much from listening to people. And all I knew was the only thing I had was honesty and openness. And it was absolutely necessary for me to declare, as terrified as I was, from the very get-go as soon as we were opening to each other, to say, "The father of my children is white." And what that meant in Tougaloo to those young black people then, and to deal with it, to talk about myself openly, to deal with their hostility, their sense of disillusionment, to come past that, was very hard.

It was through poetry that we began to deal with these things—formally, I knew nothing. Adrienne, I had never read a book *about* poetry! Never read a book about poetry. I picked up one day a book by Karl Shapiro—a little thin white book. I opened it and something he said made sense. It was, "Poetry doesn't make Cadillacs." That was a symbol for all the things I was—yes. So I would talk to the students, and I was learning. It was the first time I'd ever talked about writing, because always before I'd listened—part of my being inarticulate, inscrutable, because I didn't understand in terms of verbalization, and if I did I was too terrified to speak anyway. But at Tougaloo *we* talked about poetry. And I got the first copies of my book there at Tougaloo. I had never been in this relationship with black people before. Never. There had been a very uneasy dialogue between me and the Harlem Writers Guild, where I felt I was tolerated but never really accepted—that I was both crazy and queer but

would grow out of it all. Johnny Clarke adopted me because he really loved me, and he's a kind man, you know? And he taught me wonderful things about Africa. And he said to me, "You are a poet. You *are* a poet. I don't understand your poetry but you are a poet, you are." So I would get this underlining of me. "You're not doing what you're supposed to do, but, yes, you can do it and we totally expect you to. You are a bright and shining light. You're off on a lot of wrong turns—women, the Village, white people—all of this, but you're young yet. You'll find your way." So I would get these double messages. This kind of underlining and rejection at the same time—it reduplicated my family, you see. In my family it was: You're a Lorde, so that makes you special and particular above anybody else in the world. But you're not our kind of Lorde, so when are you going to straighten up and act right?

Question: And so Tougaloo was an entirely different experience of working with other black writers.

AL: When I went to Tougaloo, I didn't know where, what, to give, where it was going to come from. I knew I couldn't give what regular teachers of poetry give, nor did I want to, because they'd never served me. I couldn't give what English teachers give. The only thing I had to give was me. And I was so involved with these young people—I really loved them. I knew the emotional life of each of those students because we would have conferences, and that became inseparable from their poetry. And I would talk to them in the group about their poetry in terms of what I knew about their lives, and that there was a real connection between the two, that was inseparable no matter what they'd been taught to the contrary.

I knew by the time I left Tougaloo that teaching was the work I needed to be doing, that library work—by this time I was head librarian at the Town School—being a librarian was not enough. It had been very satisfying to me. And I had a kind of stature I hadn't had before in terms of working. But from the time I went to Tougaloo and did that workshop, I knew: not only, yes, I am a poet, but also, this is the kind of work I'm going to do.

*

At John Jay Colege one of the attempts to discredit me among black students was to say I was a lesbian. Now, by this time, I would have considered myself uncloseted, but I had never discussed my own poetry at John Jay, nor my sexuality. I knew, as I had always known, that the only way you can head people off from using who you are against you is to be honest and open first, to talk about yourself before they talk about you. It wasn't even courage—it was a protective mechanism for myself, this speaking up, like publishing "Love Poem" in *Ms.* in 1971 and bringing it in and putting it up on the wall of the English Department.

Question: I remember hearing you read "Love Poem" on the Upper West Side, a coffeehouse at 72nd Street. It was the first time I'd heard you read it. It was incredible. Like defiance. It was glorious.

AL: That's how I was feeling. I was always feeling my back against the wall, because, as bad as it is now, the idea of open lesbianism in the black community was—I mean, we've moved miles in a very short time. But in the early seventies it was totally horrible. My publisher called and literally said he didn't understand the words of "Love Poem." He said, "Now what is this all about, are you supposed to be a man?" And he was a poet! And I said, "No, I'm loving a woman."

*

Question: In "Poems Are Not Luxuries," you wrote: "The white fathers told us, 'I think; therefore I am,' and the black mothers in each of us—the poets—whisper in our dreams, 'I feel; therefore I can be free.'" I've heard it remarked that here you are simply restating the old stereotype of the rational white male and the emotional dark female. I believe you were saying something very different, but could you talk a little about that?

AL: There are a couple of things. I have heard that accusation, that I'm contributing to the stereotype, that I'm saying the province of intelligence and rationality belongs to the white male. But that is like—if you're travelling a road that begins nowhere and ends nowhere, the ownership of that road is meaningless. If you have no land out of

which the road comes, no place that road goes to, geographically, no goal, then the existence of that road is totally meaningless. So to say that we're leaving rationality to the white man is like leaving to him a piece of that road that begins nowhere and ends nowhere. When I talk about the black mothers in each of us, the poets, I don't mean the black mothers in each of us who are called poets, I mean the black mother—

Question: Who *is* the poet?

AL: The black mother who is the poet in every one of us. Now when males, or patriarchal thinking whether it's male or female, reject that combination, then we're truncated. Rationality is not unnecessary. It serves the chaos of knowledge. It serves feeling. It serves to get from some place to some place. And if you don't honor those places, then the road is meaningless. Too often, that's what happens with intellect and rationality and a certain kind of circular, academic, analytic thinking. But, ultimately, I don't see feel/think as a dichotomy. I see them as a choice of ways and combinations.

Do you realize, we've come full circle, because we're talking about the point where knowing and understanding mesh. What understanding begins to do is to make knowledge available for use, and that's the urgency, that's the push, that's the drive. I don't know how I wrote the long prose piece [in process] but I just knew that I had to do it.

Question: That you had to understand what you knew, and also make it available to others?

AL: That's right. Inseparable process now. But for me, I had to know I knew it first—I had to feel.

Lynda Koolish

ADRIENNE RICH has authored eleven books of poetry and two of prose. She has taught, lectured, and read her work at many colleges and universities here and abroad. She is a lesbian feminist and lives in Massachusetts. For the past decade Rich's life and work have been increasingly committed to and affected by radical feminism. W. W. Norton, her publisher, has issued her most recent poetry book, *A Wild Patience Has Taken Me This Far: Poems 1978–1981.*

Audre Lorde: Biographical Notes

I am a black woman warrior poet doing my work.

For poets and other live human beings, those designations used to widen and expand identity are precious, but those categories used to restrict or narrow identity are death.

In the interests of expanding identities, poetic and otherwise, you can say Lorde is woman, black, lesbian, urban, mother, cantankerous, warrior, revolutionary, uppity, feminist, and fat—all precious and inseparable aspects of my living that infuse energy into my work.

I write as I live, teach, love, garden, etc.—with the absolute conviciton that all my activities are only different faces of the same task, surviving and spreading the word (teaching as a survival skill, the task facing all of us). By us I mean those who are moving through the categories used to divide us toward an acceptance of the creative need for human difference and the value of change.

It is this acceptance and the willingness to defend it which, I believe, are the cornerstones of creativity and growth.

As for history and the daily tasks at hand, I was born in the middle of Harlem in New York City in the middle of the last depression. I write with my toes curled up very tightly and one eye always on the nearest exit.

AUDRE LORDE

*

In 1976 Audre Lorde was invited as the American observer to the African-Asian International Writers' Conference held in Moscow and Tashkent, USSR. In 1977 she was one of the American artists invited to participate in FESTAC, the Second World Black and African Festival of Arts and Culture, held in Lagos, Nigeria. She has received many other honors, among them two National Endowment for the Arts grants (1968, 1981–82) and two New York Creative Artists' Public Service Award grants (1972, 1976).

In addition to her writing and editing activities, Audre Lorde is a professor of English and creative writing at John Jay College of Criminal Justice, of The City University of New York. As a personal note, she has two children at home.

Currently, she is an advisory editor of *Black Scholar* magazine and a contributing editor of *Black Box* magazine. Recent major writing activities include the completing of her first novel, *I've Been Standing on This Streetcorner a Hell of a Long Time!*, and a series of essays on breast cancer and American women, titled "Power vs. Prostheses."

Audre Lorde's poetry has appeared in many anthologies and periodicals. Most recently, these have included *Essence*, *The Iowa Review*, *The Massachusetts Review*, *Ms.*, *Women Poems*, *The New Yorker*, and *13th Moon*.

Her third book of poetry, *From a Land Where Other People Live* (Broadside Press), was nominated for a National Book Award in Poetry in 1973. Her other books of poetry include: *New York Head Shop and Museum* (Broadside Press); *Coal* (W. W. Norton & Co.); *Between Our Selves* (Eidolon Editions); and *The Black Unicorn* (W. W. Norton & Co., 1978). Her 1980 collection of original essays, *Cancer Journals*, was published by Spinsters, Ink.

Judith Johnson Sherwin

NEW YORK, NEW YORK

Miranda's Birthspell

in a redwalled cave, tied down
on a frame, hard pressed, pressing hard to get you out,
in pain and afraid of pain, protected from unclean
hands and all ills but pain and the fear of pain,
my heart pumps blood for you and I promise you again:
tomorrow I'll hold an ear of corn over your head till your thoughts leap
like a field in flower, make you suck sugar till your words run sweet;
you'll take honey in your hands and happiness will stick to your palm;
you'll suffer no want, for I'll go buy you dimestore pearls,
jewels you'll fling in the gutter as if born to worlds of wealth.

in the redwalled cave
where I count the dangers that cradle you, I am not myself.
I am one with all women in bloodprint and birthpit who twisted
good spells, bad spells, and waited for their blood to run free.
in that space before history my mind is not my mind
but the mind of an animal / outside all known rule.
tomorrow I'll rub your fingers with roasted spiders
and those fine ashes will run nimbly over music and human hearts;
skin of sleek snake will slide over your skin so lightly
anyone who tries to hold you will find it hard.
hair of hornless beast will blend with your hair so easily
you shall shake off all hunters.

in the redwalled cave
where I crouch with you in a task of tearing, I see
time strings the eyes of waiting dangers brighter than beads to a kill,
knits up the knucklejoints, knots in a noose for you to tell;
the water breaks hot on my thighs and I count my tears.
remember always, what was one thing can never break. you are trapped in me,
bound to me forever, as I to my mother, by a cord of force
which thins to invisible but pulls like the sun.
I bear witness my body continues to feel with the flesh I lose:
my child, my parasite which has swollen my blood,

my unknown life, my secret light that will out, my strength, when you bleed
fourteen years from now in another world, this stay-at-home blood
in this body, this cave, this cell, this emptying self
shall feel that pull, and clot to an unseen wound.

how shall I keep you safe once I let you go?
I must learn to protect my blood, when you wake to smooth
your shape from the sheets, when you walk to sweep out your prints
so no enemy can plant stone to bruise, glass to cut,
when you pierce hand or foot with a nail to scrub that nail
every day until your wound heals and infection dies,
starved of your blood on its iron. I must teach you wisdom
to choose your pain, to be hurt by no unclean thing.

> confined in this redveined cell, locked up in my life
> with you locked in me and forcing your passage out,
> I twist with you in our pain, I shout aloud
> to the predators where they wait, as the blood spouts
> from the womb which must shield you and drop you and has no choice:
> *the blood and the tears are the life / no way out of that tide.*

what wisdom can hold such a tumble? tomorrow evening
shall I shake the lid of a pot over your closed eyes
till the drops condensed there wet your cheeks and cheat time,
and your tears are all spent young? before nightfall toil
after each trace you scatter, child prodigal
of shed clothes, teeth, hair, nails, print of foot and body?
what a Mother's Day of pains I shall celebrate
picking up after you: your hale life's trail:
leavings of food, one flesh with the food you have eaten,
the point that pierces you polished, the cord underground,
no shred left! unmarked, leaving no mark,
you shall push through these straits a frozen stream, delivered
from blood in blood and still not free of our blood.

> this, then, is the labor, the hard act of birth:
> not to push you out of this cave or out of this body,
> but to get you out of myself, my love's strength,
> my fear which stops the channel against all life
> in the name of safety and motherhood and love,
> push you out of all shelter, riding our common bloodtide
> into enemy hands. your head has just sliced through me.
> I must let you slide out in the exile that fills our morning;
> the hard air cuts us both.

dear, almost born,
bruised with your fight to elbow your passage through me,
I bear witness your body must feel with the flesh you lose:
the mill of your nine months' turning under my heartbeat
grinds out still, as the falls pull the stream through the millrace,

birth after birth in gouts that clot and shake free,
as the hollow womb shrinks / keeps the print of fullness.

though the hairs on my head be numbered, those I have sown
on comb or pillow shall leap up to witness me,
not veil, not helmet, eclipse, but unseen corona.
measure: the blood I pump out now with you
is more than can fill my body. let me drop all fear for you
with a calm pressure of strength, as my voice shouts now
and the birth yell, resonant, fills this room between shouts,
as our cut hair will guard our heads in a radiance of force,
as our cast nails will mark deep, as our blood when it clots
still links the wound to the flow.

      in this redwalled room
      where together we strain towards breath, as we shall in our time
      strain away from each other, the sponge from the cord and not break,
      in this hollow hold in ourselves where the predators wait
      sure in a foretaste of blood, where you swim and climb
      and wrestle my flesh away, bear witness now
how we cast away our lifeline in making this birth
and the line still holds, how surely you ride out the tide,
how you make the air yours with your welcome, triumphant cry,
how the tears that were mine are yours and hold us fast,
you who are mine and not mine and my daughter at last.

Robin Morgan

NEW YORK, NEW YORK

Gilda Grillo

Documentary

Based on the documentary film
River of Sand, by Robert Gardner,
a Phoenix Productions Film
from Harvard University, aired
on Channel 13, August 25, 1977.

The Hamar of Southwest Ethiopia
are the subject.

But too much stands between us and this
stone-age people—an alien tribe, a dying culture,
and a geographical distance great
even in these days of Concorde.

But she is—how old? Not
an elder, for without standing
as an elder (she's a woman). No,
there is nothing which does not
stand between us.

"One keeps going," she says,
squatting, brushing
at the flies that return to her face.
"When a son
is born, the father gives him a gun.
When a girl is born, the father
gives her leg irons.
It's not just me." She says this.
She laughs but never smiles.

"Your father wars and gives you away.
Nobody sees you. Where can you go?
You enter your husband's house
a girlchild with only your rings as your own:

leg rings, rattling
arm rings. Your skirt is taken away.
In your newness you are afraid
of him. You become
of his people."

She says this.
I say, "Everything stands surely
between us, you and I, we—"

She describes a ceremony:
"*now he is old enough to beat women and girls,
to hunt, now he is a new man. Babies
beat dogs, men beat women;
cattle wear bells, women wear bracelets,
you control yourself and go on.*"

All her front teeth have been torn
out. "When I was circumcised, you understand."
She says this. She uses the word
"circumcision," not "clitoridectomy," not
naming the sharpened shell that carved
        out the clitoris,
the excision of pleasure, the scream that is proof of
womanhood, not
speaking the word "infibulation," the sewing
up of the labia, leaving one
hole for urine and pus and menstrual fluid
to seep through, or the then forced
tearing open to ensure him
virginity, loyalty, tightness.
She does not say this. I
say this,
and I say, "What more
what more could possibly
stand between us, what—"

the rattle of sand underfoot, *the rattle*
the rattle of iron bracelets
     "for decoration and for bondage"
she says this
the rattle of teeth into a wooden bowl
the rattle *nothing*
stands between

"Women look best when scarred," she says they say.
There are scars on her belly. She says,
"Women carry the scars earned by men for killing
an enemy. Men do not scarify themselves
    —they build
headdresses of clay and ostrich feathers
    and decorate
these, but they do not scar their own flesh.
It is for women to carry their scars."
She is actually bitter. She dares to be
bitter, she laughs and snarls
at her own tribe, at the camera,
she rattles like a desert snake nothing
stands surely.

"You are beaten," she says. "*You are
    beaten as your mother was beaten.
    You are ground beneath the grinding stone.
      The rattle
    of small drums, the rattle
    of wire whips, of iron bracelets.
    The crunch of sorghum on the grinding stone,
      the rhythm.*"
    "He is
beating you even when he is not," she says.
"His whip is always in his hand, and when you run
he only sits. Where could you go? I cannot
marry again." Nothing stands
everything stands everything between I am not

"You become reconciled, and that is that. Then
the husband will leave you alone." She says
    this aloud.
    *You are ground. You are ground beneath
    the grinding stone,
    you are beaten, you look best when scarred,
    you are
    a rattle in a new man's hand. Nothing
    is bad, how
    can it be bad?*
"Do women have erections or go cattle raiding

or hunting?" She laughs. "Do women have
    erections or kill?
No," she rattles, "women work. Women kill lice
until the sun sets; that is how we raid. Women
get wood and go home, women
haul water and work the sorghum field. That is
how a woman hunts. You stay. You grind
    the sorghum stone,
    *you are the grinding stone. You
    touch your children and you stay.*"
Nothing
rattles between. Everything *rat
tles*, "I cannot be
her. You cannot
surely

"Men own beehives and collect honey. The leg rings
of a woman are like new beehives in a tree:
    they look so fine
and new," she says they say this. She says,
    "*You become of his people. Nobody sees
    you. How can it be
    bad? Where can you go?*
Men sit on stools, drink from gourds.
Women sit on the ground. After the first
birth your husband will say, 'A child
has come from between us. Shall I beat you
then forever?'"

I am not you
are not surely cannot be
we are
    "*Who does not
    in this world practice slavery?*"
    She laughs, the toothless sophisticate.
    "*How can it be
    bad? Nobody sees you.
Now he is old enough to be
a man, to beat women to show his love,*"
she unsmiles. "*A woman may be whipped only
by a man of the clan into which she will marry.
We are not savages,*" she rattles.

    We are
not the subject, you and I. I say
this. We are not a stone-age people. We at least
try surely everything stands be
    *Men jump cows, drink blood, suck marrow,
    pray for the desert flooding.*

"May all be well," men say
   and spit upon the ground to make it ripe.
Women are to be whipped, to work, to die,
to look best when scarred, to become resigned
into freedom where he cannot follow her death *I am*
      not the same, I am not

the subject

When you die, they will butter your corpse
and fold it like a fetus, naked, into the hole.
Your husband's oldest brother leads the ritual,
and lays heavy stones across the grave. You will not
escape. Whips
from the barasá tree are cut and strewn
above your body
      to control your vengeance.
A kid is sacrificed, especially when
you die in childbirth.
Your corpse is buttered with blood.

      You and I have
nothing in common. Everything
everything stands I refuse
nothing not a stone-age we are surely

"You are beaten as your mother was beaten," she
      sings.
      You are ground beneath the grinding stone,
      you are sorghum and stone, you are ground.
      How can it be wrong, nobody sees you,
it isn't just me
      you are ground as your mother was ground,
      you control
yourself,
      you touch
      the child and go on,
      you become of his people, you stay,
      cattle wear bells, women wear irons,
you stay
      The rattle of her voice, the rattle
      of iron bracelets,
of teeth into a bowl of laughter, the rattle
of a coiled snake, of shell against pelvic bone,
the scream of womanhood, the rattle
of chaff against a stone. The rattle
      in my throat.

No   distance.
No barrier between.   Nothing

stands between us.

As your mother was beaten.
As my mother was beaten.
      No distance. No distance traveled?
Nothing stands behind us.

Who does not in this world practice slavery?
      No map, no model.
Nothing stands before us.

The Hamar of Southwest Ethiopia
      are   not the subject.

Lunch Hour

(for Isabel Bishop)

Only the fastidiously unheroic dare
to incomplete the unmiraculous—
which is a scrim for saying what
we who figure on the ground
of slums like these learn early,
or late, to recognize: this average radiance,
coarse as hope, that moves us
to light, however briefly, on that sticky web
of grace through which we are enseamed.
Forget, forget how the grain of you daily
grits against pearl air. Consider the space
made yours behind the brush-strokes;
shoulders can slump here, spines can question,
knees relax apart. Intimate
as gauze blotting a wound,
this pleasure tenders you a confidence
stolen with permission, a sweet
shared as it melts, like understanding
or like tragedy. And in the face
of this, an ignorant smile
may redefine transparency, outrace
the speed of shade, and bless even the noon
that cottons in again to spread its fungal haze
between, between. So, unremembered and unseen,
love's art persists in beveling back what is
apparently so real—the epic shopgirl and
      stenographer
at last unhumbled, undisguised, appear—
Beatrice and Gemma in Union Square.

Jane Miller

PLAINFIELD, VERMONT

Lightning Storm

"the voluptuousness of misery"
MACHADO DE ASSIS

The morning of your departure, off-handed and passionate,
brings the trees too close to the house. Yes, my young lyric,
heavy with yourself and joined by unparalleled jealousy
to grief, you live suddenly, you thrash and dream.

Yet again your sensitive hearing pours the bright claret
of self-hate into its trough. Drunk on the sound
of your life without metaphor, superior, desirable, detached,
betrayed: a shadow against a green lawn. The impotent figure

all voice, not otherwise sexually exposed, wears a commonplace
and sad vanity. Fantasy abhors a face. It was nostalgia,
not the body you had in mind. A horse's ribbed side
unabashedly flexes in the heat. You begin walking again

but more slowly, with no more heart than a word, one
tree unleafed, and on your back the strong high instep and red lacquered
nails of the sun. The intrusion of a few phrases of a foreign
language, panoramic, fringes a sky that is always blue

for those with wings. You have been down and photographed every woman
you had: almond eyes like nooses. Vertiginous desire that tired
your lovers, until not even you this morning suffer
the rain falling violently now, no, please, not into

the properly humbled attitude. You find yourself going home.
These so, these irresistible interiors, like gardens run to seed
alternately soak and burn. No one is sentimental.
Not one of these flashes is for you.

6 a.m.

I want to be bad, but I'm not. There's a warm breath
off the bridle path. The last groans of sex recede, light
musk on a woman's wrist. A sudden clearing. Birds, almost,
where I'm out walking. This season's animals? We're beginners
making tracks: I'm proving how at last you meet and turn
him away. The wilderness you walk out of is thawing, different
by day, by night: that incredible story of the man you waited for.
Cats stir sleepers at this hour. Your son gets up to pee.
My body retraces the last time, tenderly, it had no desire

to be understood, like a nose-bleed. The sexually responsive
ground-swell is a form in which we see our excess, cryptically.
Tobogganers will slide right by here later, hair held by cold
barrettes, the intimacy of hearts and hard ground. Not for you
alone the clock-radio prepares *when I look into your blue skies, baby. . .* —
I'm also in a dream, exaggerating early morning moans, the way
earth hardens, opens, runs. Skunk spray's next; snowstorms
demystified to rain. Drift, love; the hands haven't yet signaled
with their bloody tips.

5 a.m.

Spicier. The best thing would be snow, and soon.
Twice the water has frozen because there's no
ground cover. I wake to let the tap drip, get cold
cider and decide to dress. I'll have to bank the
pipes with styrofoam and straw. Released, it's un-
expectedly warm. Ice thins to isinglass. I pace,
I take our last taut gratuitous embrace and fling
myself into the slush. Guilty over two lovers in one
week, I dirty the gravel with abandon. Then a crow's
humiliating *flock, flock.*

       Smoke backing up
and belching. I watch the house. Night nightens
on its way to the shortest day of the year.
The door is gusted shut and my eyes dark, my brief
body that contains the future. How long am I
willing to wait? I see now the months and years,
interiors in blue, in pale, in bed. Is it to end
nobly that we lie down for so long dying
to be touched there, and there? How well I look, and you
and you and you. Foul, I help myself to friends.

The Long Fingers of *1956*

Mercy kept me out of the river.
Colder still, the air
burned my young ass.
At night I flew, a cramped
left side, both hands
over my head, the river looked good
down there. A canoe flipped
Abby and me into its empty brace
once. I held on,
fingers long gone blue. Grampa died
for nothing one shining afternoon:
no one to start his heart. Pity

and fury aside, who was supposed
to be there wasn't. They told me
September, the last day
in September in the bathroom, home.
Goddamn them. He should be here
lovers stars the owl spread in the pond
they're all supposed to be here holding on
the side of moon the living
cling to. What descends effortlessly
through the chestnut leaves? Distant
star, skinny kid seven, grown
homesick in Vermont tonight
hoist two hands overhead for me, for you
not giving in, flying.

Colette Inez

NEW YORK, NEW YORK

Mary Dermody

Reading da Leaves

what do you want
gimme a little something
before I start

you gonna write a lucky poem
that make you rich
in da dark I see big ship
you gonna meet this moviestar

I see in da leaves
you gonna have long journey
in da fall da jackpot is yours
because of da poem

wait I see your poem on TV

you got a hit show
gods gotta make it right
gimme a little more

my mother got a bad heart
I can tell by your hand
you da kind of person
like to have fun with your brains

the moviestar is gonna love you
I see romance
you gonna read him da poem
but he got a bad heart

and has an attack
then you get an idea for this big poem
I don't have change for a ten
its gonna be okay

Carol Muske

NEW YORK, NEW YORK

Chapter One

You said it over the top of the book,
you said it softly: *No no*

in disbelief, the way the heroine cries
no in a later chapter, as it dawns on her
who she is and why she is in this book.

And the novel left open to the murder scene
lets the murder scene be altered gradually
by the light from the window—so the killer
will bring the axe down on her skull

against the light blue sky forming at the edge
of the page. Never again will print betray you
like this. Never again will your hands travel
with hers along the blind margins, grasp

the gunwales of the invented rowboat, gather
the oars like crutches, limping up the black pond

into another plot. *It will be sunny all day today.*

It will be sunny tomorrow. I can't go anywhere
unless someone writes it first. Everyday I dust,
and my mother shoves the Hoover around in a huff.
Like her, I have someone dying on my hands and

the sun sits completely down on the coffee table,
on a crystal ball—and the wax rose inside
refuses to close or open. I can write it now:

how the rising dust occurred to me like the
thought of crime, how I didn't expect to be
forgiven as I picked it up and shook the sleeping
hurricane. So slowly at first my mother didn't notice

the wax rose blowing authorless away
    from the dustcloth,
the unchristened bitch rising up chapter by chapter
to throw it out—the ending, the beginning,
the unwritten heavens already opening to receive her.

Special Delivery to Curtis:
The Future of the World

The sky over Cyprus is blue
and usual. And you want me to move there for
politics. Believe me, the sky over Manhattan
is white. Everyday the same parade passes on
Fifth Avenue.

And even if we could demonstrate,
join hands as far downtown as that last bar,
our lives would not try convention.

What women we are! One drink and
the radio's topical nonsense makes sense, the
way destiny appeals to the hopeless. That's
politics.

And I take no pride in circumstance.
There's an ambitious biography writing itself in
my future having to do with the dirty white pros-
cenium of the park and the occasion it frames: two
women, a traffic light stuck on red.

I'm a feminist. There are the lives
we need to survive and those we don't. Of course,
everyone loves a crippled debutante. Everyone loves
a calendar. Did you say it was Wednesday? *I'm a
feminist.* Don't take that chair, we're expecting
a feminist. Is there life after rhetoric?

No. Just this moment. Two women.
The future of the world. And this poor light
holding the only crown it owns over your
        incomparable
profile, the brilliant manifesto of your hair.

Sonya Dorman

WEST MYSTIC, CONNECTICUT

Sherri Dorman

Two Poets on the Way to the Palace

We push our raft out on the river
between low banks, the water hissing
a welcome. We want to travel light as we do
in dreams, taking nothing but our lives.

At first, trains rattle beside us, but
we're easily outrun. Hills of wild lilac
rise on both sides. We take turns
poling the meander and flow, she snoozes
when I guide. Soon, I'll sprawl a while
undisturbed by more than beauty.

Sliding under high iron bridges
that join factory towns, we hear
the looms hum out their miles of cloth.
A few thin children, unsmiling, wave
from shore. Grey papers flutter down
in place of moths and blue herons,
pasting themselves to our sides.

At night we tie up to a littered shore
not far from a city's glow. Trucks grind
through our sleep. What did we expect?
We dream robbers who strut toward us
masked, whirling bicycle chains.

After days on the water our raft is sodden.
The river narrows, darkening, below huge peaks,
and no one waves from the cold ravines.
This is the high part of the country.
"Listen," she says, "don't you hear it?"

When she lifts the pole it drips
soundless drops, invisible stones.

The swift current drinks them. Our hearts
surge like hooked fish as we're rushed
toward the palace's roaring brink.

Whodunit

If he bores her, always falling
on his sword, she doesn't say so.
Last she looked, the sword
was on the wall, only decor,
dulled, pitted, a souvenir
of the last five wars.

Her reach isn't long enough
to dust a blade slung
above the hearth's black mouth.
She carries in wood enough,
though, from the porch.

Leaning her head into the maw,
into the cold chimney breath
smelling of ashes and char,
her arms are able, laying
sticks on, settling a big log
at the back, anticipating fire.

Above the mantel the weapon
is just part of the wall.
When she bothers to observe it
she's surprised how the hilt
shines clean from the center
of his chest, how his eyelids flicker
in the red light from her forge.

35

Judith Moffett

MEDIA, PENNSYLVANIA

"Cambridge University Swimming Club / No Public Access to River"

I

Members in their seventies fail to recall
a filthier July. Mildew rots the roses
before they open, the wet wind hurts. Finally,
so rarely, reprieve—dissolving turquoise sky
poured from a honeypot, a week's ration of summer
condensed in a day. This dazzling morning
the club lures and subverts, druglike. Work?
How could any of us keep, or go, away?

At Sheep's Green, where the public swim,
shrieking bodies clog the numbing river;
boats hazard a way among them and pole upstream.
Picnic hampers, guitars. Half a mile and they'll
glide past our little greensward, their three or four
necks craning: a naughty glimpse of Eden! Adam
and Eve, though, are winding themselves in towels.
It might be Mrs. Grundy. It might be the Law.

Still, these rare aqua days, we grow careless.
Come ahead, boats. Too much bother, hastily
splashing out of the effervescent Cam
every couple of minutes and for what?
Deep under chestnut tassles and skeleton elms,
screened by rank goldenrod and a straggle of privet,
we sprawl on dandelions in bliss. The palest
sunshafts made us addicts; these suffuse us.

Again and again we rise and enter the river.

II

No punts in view, no paddlers? Good.
—Nip down four treads
Of weathered wood
And slime, and plunge away. I swim
Breast stroke carefully so my head's
Held out, above the dubious skim,

Perhaps of oil, like that on tea
Cooled in the pot.
Ahead, my vee-
shaped strokes part flotsam: nameless muck
Stirred up by punt-poles from the bot-
tom, algae, sticks, leaves, petals. Yuck.

The winds that skim the surface clear
Elsewhere, fall foul
Of tall trees here.
Not for the squeamish, this. Indeed
I've more than once choked back a howl,
Clutched round the ankle by some weed.

But Cam feels lovelier than she looks
Close-to, and teeming
Swans and ducks,
Ducklings, cygnets, and schools of dace
Proclaim her waters safe for swimming
(If not for putting in your face).

This year the city's closed Sheep's Green.
"Admission Free,
Risk Yours" they mean,
Like cigarettes; yet what a throng!
Club stalwarts who with unfeigned glee
Take lunchtime dips all winter long

36

Don't die, what's more, and they *dive* in!
Time was, however . . .
Let's let Gwen

Raverat, Darwin grandchild, tell.
As an old lady, Mrs. Raver-
at could still "remember the smell

very well, for all the sewage went into the river, till the town was
at last properly drained, when I was about ten years old. There is
a tale of Queen Victoria being shown over Trinity by the Master, Dr.
Whewall, and saying, as she looked down over the bridge: 'What are all
those pieces of paper floating down the river?' To which, with
great presence of mind, he replied: 'Those, ma'am, are notices that
bathing is forbidden.' However, we lived at the upper end of town,
so it was not so very bad. That was why the bathing places were on the
upper river, on Sheep's Green and Coe Fen."

This was the 1890's. Gwen again:

III

"All summer, Sheep's Green and Coe Fen were pink with boys, as naked
as God made them; for bathing drawers did not exist then; or , at
least, not on Sheep's Green. You could see the pinkness, dancing
about, quite plain, from the end of our Big Island. Now to go Up the
River, the goal of all the best picnics, the boats had to go right
by the bathing places, which lay on both sides of the narrow stream.
These dangerous straits were taken in silence, and at full speed.
The Gentlemen were set to the oars—in this context one obviously thinks
of them as Gentlemen—and each Lady unfurled a parasol, and, like an
ostrich, buried her head in it, and gazed earnestly into its silky
depths, until the crisis was past, and the river was decent again."

—if only they'd do it now, what a lot of trouble
all concerned would be saved! the bathers who, cursing,
must scoot for cover each time another flat prow
pushes beyond the bend; the sad little flasher
who climbs the fence and crackles in the bushes
waiting to prance out, madly waving his penis,
at the first boat with a woman aboard; the woman,
her outing spoiled, who then must file a complaint;
the policeman who must cycle down here, take names,
try to arrest somebody; and the boaters
fled from, thwarted, never allowed to ogle—

though businessmen, clerks, writers, dons and students,
laborers, civil servants, engineers,
one archeologist, one librarian, and,
on really nice days, the tart old Dean of Pembroke,
stretched out on towels, small piles of clothes beside them,

napping, chatting, busy with books and papers,
sixty-year age span, scrawny to fit to fat,
naked of course (not counting glasses), otherwise
too ordinary for words and nearly all male—
a company which relaxes and delights me
as none has yet—should be ogled a certain way . . .

IV
Each
is personal as a thumbprint.
Soon, you know your friends' exactly
the way you know
their eyes, or hands, or height.

Whenever the elusive sun
shines, a flower-garden profusion
blooms mid-daily here, a lush display
of lolling Roman limbs and unconfinement, filling
the gaze, so rich and various,
so much to see

and everywhere in motion:
wobble of standing
languid fishflop of rolling-over
cumbrous swing of striding.
A subtle thickening, lengthening, relapsing
tones our companionship,

and the riveting changes
gravity and pushups ring on what was lately
shriveled in the cold river
were waked by idle talk
in what's now quarter-inching darkly
along a sunflushed thigh in curls,
slowly pulling a sweater on over its head.

I'm fascinated.
This garden-variety talent ever
seems a form of true
sorcery, some part held in common by
the bottled djinn, Clark Kent in public, the werewolf
under the new moon:

shape-shifters,
their powers in check; the changing prodigious,

the changing back no less.

Unassumingly, a shaftless button
cloaks a dagger. Oh, but
look! For now the cloak slits open,
the dagger slides thrillingly in its sheath . . .

Yet because we're so
precarious really, safe together only
within a membrane
too easily torn and just beneath eggshell, because
we mutually acknowledge
this, without words,
the subject of Danish films or Dutch beaches
is dropped. Almost unseen
pulses had quickened, but not much.
Beneath my skin
a tiny buzzing vibrator had begun
its friendly nuzzling, but does not
insist.

So we subside in sunshine. Truly,
this is bliss:
to bask here, daisy amid sunflowers,
strand among other strands
in a plain web of titillation and trust,
noticing everything, agreeably
nattering on about politics—work—food—
the filthy weather, no summer this year . . .

Marie Ponsot

JAMAICA, NEW YORK

Franzis von Stechow

Half-Life: Copies to All Concerned

Gentlemen: how are you? Here things go well.
I write you after these many years to ask
If you have any news of all I lost
That I'd forwarded to you, insured, I'd thought,
First Class, on urgent demand, with a good
Guarantee (though that would be expired now).

What I miss is not you (as you do, now?)
but the girl I gave you. Did she do well,
That stern young person planning to be good,
Sure of her dress, her footing, her right to ask?
Lovers have half-life in each other's thought
Long after; is the mark she made quite lost?

Have you traces of her? That she got lost
I'd never guessed; but from what I hear now,
You never quite received her, though we thought
She knew more than the directions well
And would get by, skilled in what not to ask.
Were her efforts at lipstick any good?

Did she learn to tell bad eagerness from good?
If you do remember her, then she's not lost;
I've forgotten her so long I must ask
(I didn't love her then as I might now)
What, for a while, told you you knew her well,
What live cry for her survives in your thought,

Who she was for you, what she meant, feared,
      thought.
She had trunks, jammed with what her love judged
      good;
Are they still somewhere, tagged & indexed well,
Or are they, like my pictures of her, lost?
I've saved what she left—stale or fragile now—
Latin books, laughs, wine, lists of what to ask.

Should you have questions, do feel free to ask,
Given the always present tense of thought.
Though I know no time is as bad as now,
Recall her you—I could!—let him make good
The tale of that naked pure young fool, lost
Before I got a chance to know her well.

I should say, as well: beyond what I ask

Lies the you you lost, alive; in my thought
still planning to be good. Redeem him now.

Now ask your thought for this lost good. Farewell.

"Sois Sage O Ma Douleur"

I

Here they are, what you hid,
what shamed you, the
secrets of your life in cardboard
cartons at my feet (your
life you laid no claim to)
gifts, accomplishments, genius,
and what you did with these.

Here is the cast-off evidence,
amassed, earned, dry—
I read aghast through thousands
of pages of claims
you earned and hid and
did not choose to make
or did not make
or no one heard you make

                while you made
dinner, jokes, love, kids'
tuition money, friends, the most
of dim situations,
and the best of everything.

You are extreme, being you & dead,
your beginning & end extremely visible;
but the dereliction of your crowded cartons
many women know
(and some men
who live like younger
sons or girls or saints—
but most who expect nothing
for work well done
are women) especially
women of my generation
—almost famous almost exemplary
almost doctors almost presidents almost
powerful, women entirely
remarkable, entirely unremarked,

women with dues paid
who lay no claim to what they've paid for
and are ashamed
to be ashamed to lay a claim.

I cry telling a woman (like you but
like me still alive, taking that chance)
of your secret works and unbanked treasury.
Redfaced I blow my nose & we
exchange stares, her face stripped by insight
back from forty to fourteen; she knows;
the rose-petal peony of her snaps in a
jump-cut back to a bud, she looks
bud-tight, slices of white petal showing,
slowest to open where there is no sun;
there is no sun; our secret is your secret;
we see what we have done.
We see your life. It hurts us.
It is our life. There are many like us.
We have daughters; they have daughters.
What are we to do?   Many
and many like us would mock us if they knew
that we who mistrust power & will not compete
          for it
conceive of other claims but only in pain conceive
that we might make them.

. . . died at fifty. Is fifty young?
It is young. You died too young.
Dead woman, this side of despair
where I use you to say I care,
does knowing what we can't help
help? or was the absence of answer
fatal, was that the infarction
that sprung your heart apart?
did the infected heart, healed, fall loose again
          helpless,
did our helplessness prevent your breath
as you lay in wait for the too-late ambulance
until you drew an answer for us with your death?

What model did we who are like you give you?
none. One of us, as good as you a scholar,
worships to complete her late husband's opera; one
slips hand to mouth modestly and paints
essential paintings, goes on painting, who
sees it? only a few; as for me I start out

but everything I encourage to happen
keeps me from finishing

I do not write your name here
because it would hurt me;
you would have hated it; you deserve
silence for failure who had
silence for your excellence.
You had got used to that, made each success
a smaller plant in a smaller garden with less light,
and concealed among its leaves the stalks of
          suffering
perfectly unbudded, the sleekest secret.

Oh, no one discouraged you; many loved you,
everyone liked you, why not, so generous, great
parties; some did blame you obscurely: why
were you—gifted, rich—not famous?
That echoed in you,
didn't it; hurt your heart;
made your breath shorten with anxious guilt.

Step by step your breathless death accuses us.
The cartons found in your attic
full of your successful procedures
accuse us whose products are like yours
kept left-handed, womanly secondary
according to the rules. Whose rules?
How can we keep our hot
hatred of power
from chilling into impotence? You
could have disbarred the rules if anyone
had noticed you in time behind them.
With your costly help can we undo
the rules and with or without shame
lay our claims?
Should we who can be happy picturing
who we are, burst alive out of that frame
in our daughters' names?
I say
I am too old, tired, crazy, cold—to
say nothing of ashamed—
to try.
At my feet
your insistent cartons, their danger
implicit, speak or sing in
tongues or invisible flames.

II

Q: Brought to book at last,
    what did you say on your day
    after death, how did you
    sum up your argument?

A: This far side of dying there is no time
    for distance, and so no irony.
    I had to be plain; I said:

I was not a success.
I buried my treasures and lost the maps,
stewardess of my obscurity.
My life was comfortable, easy;
I was lucky; my one triumph was
to experience the world as holy
and to find that humorous.

I was beautiful by strict standards
for each age; dressed well, moved well.
I did not use my beauty.
I liked to be sexual; was shy until
I gave a good partner the pleasure
of teaching me. I made no capital of sex.

I was a wife, supportive, cordial, a helpmeet
and ornament; bore healthy children, mothered
them, improvised; entertained in-laws
as God-sent; kept up our correspondence;
was a presentable hostess, a lab-sharp cook,
a welcomer. Gratefully oh gratefully
I found I was married to a friend.

I came to terms with my family inheritance,
all of it; it did not merit me anything.
I loved my brother. I saw my friends.

I was a good student; women professors
dying left me their libraries & lonely valuables;
played Chopin when asked & Rameau when alone;
had ideas; did not turn intelligence into power.

I liked parties; liked drinks with one friend,
listening; celebrated epiphany; when I was ill
the interns took coffeebreaks at my bedside

& told me their specialties;
I submitted to remedy.

Indoors my amaryllis rose yearly in crowds of
    flowers.
Blue gentians grew outside my country house,
and arbutus fragrant in early spring.
In my last years I watched the coming
and going, predictable & predictably
full of surprises, of birds
on the east-coast flyway. I understood
that they came & went of necessity yet
unaccountably, in mixed flocks, in their
various plumage, unaccountable.

I wrote stories, poems, journals, a serious novel;
no one, surely not I, saw them to praise them
enough to make them public;
I wasted my Guggenheim. My dissertation
on a fierce Frenchwoman was accepted with praises;
I did not type a clean copy, did not submit it,
was not awarded a final degree; I kept
all these papers secret, a private
joke I had no laughter for.
I wrote no reproaches.

I understood my jobs; employers cherished
their fractions of me, praised & used me.
My work was serviceable, subordinate.

I played the parts given me as
written, word-perfect; I never
laid claim to a part, do not know
what would have happened
had I laid a claim.

I was a quick study; I was not a star.

My only excuse lies in what I
observed of the birds; it is faulty;
it shouldn't apply.
Since I was not a success
I must have been a failure.
There is no one to blame
but myself.

Late

(for Marie Candee Birmingham, my mother)

I

Dark on a bright day, fear of you is two-poled,
Longing its opposite. Who were we?
What for? dreaming, I haunt you unconsoled.
Rewarded as I force thought outward, I see
A warbler, a Myrtle, marked by coin-gold—
I feel lucky, as if I'd passed a test,
And try my luck, to face the misery
Of loss on loss, find us, and give us rest.
Once we two birdwatched, eyeing shrub & tree
For the luck beyond words that was our quest;
Your rings flashing, you showed me day-holed
Owls, marsh blackbirds on red wings, the crest
Kingfishers bear. Mother, dreams are too cold
To eye the dark woodland of your bequest.

II

To eye the dark woodland of your bequest
I wear the fire of diamond on my hand,
Flawed extravagance of your first love expressed
In a many-faceted engagement band.
Recklessly cut with the blaze I invest
In my dazzling flaws, careless of weight,
The fiery cast of mind that I love planned
To sacrifice carat-points for this bright state.
It is yours still, and I go talismanned
By you to find you, though I'm lost & late.
You left this for me; ringed I go dressed
To mother us, mother, to isolate
And name the flight of what, mouth to rich breast,
We meant while we were together to create.

III

We meant while we were together to create
A larger permanence, as lovers do,
Of perfecting selves: I would imitate
By my perfections, yours; I would love you
As you me, each to the other a gate
Opening on intimate gardens and
Amiable there. Mother you were new
At it but when you looped us in the bands

Of clover hope to be each other's due,
The hope at least lasted; here I still stand
Full of the verb you had to predicate.
Though you as subject now are contraband
Half hidden, half disguised to intimidate,
I recognize your diamond on my hand.

IV

I recognize the diamond on my hand
As the imagined world where we were whole.
Now among boxed bones, pine roots, & Queens
    sand,
You have changed places with this bit of coal,
Dark to light, light to dark. To understand
The dark your child never was afraid of
I go lightless sightless birdless mole
In the dark which is half what words are made of;
I enter the dark poems memories control,
Their dark love efficient under day love.
Down I go down through the oldest unscanned
Scapes of mind to skim the dim parade
Of images long neglected lost or banned,
To root for the you I have not betrayed.

V

To root for the you I have not betrayed
I hunt the ovenbird we never found—
Or guessed we'd found when something leafbrown
    strayed
Under the trees where soft leaves lay year round.
When you'd said, "Hush," and we'd obeyed (obeyed
Lifelong too long) "Tea/cher!" we heard; the shy
Bird spoke itself, "Tea/cher!" from the dim ground
The call came plain enough to recognize
And we went out following the sound.
It went before us in the dusk; its cries
Go before me now, swerve & dip in shade
Woman daughter bird teacher teach me. Skies
Boughs brush tufts; blind I have lost where we
    played
All trust in love, to the dark of your disguise.

VI

Trust in love lost to the dark of your disguise,
I forget if I loved you; I forget

If, when I failed, you requisitioned lies;
Did we make believe we saw the bird, and set
On my lifelong list what my long life denies:
That we found what we wanted side by side?
But I did see you bird I see you yet
Your live glance glinting from leafdust; you hide
Calling, colorless, your brief alphabet
Sharp. Wait, wait for me. Flash past, dusty bride,
Stand safe, rosefooted, before my finite eyes.
Sing, undeafen me. Bird be identified.
Speak yourself. I dread love that mystifies.
Say we wanted what we found side by side.

VII

I say I wanted what I found at your side.
("Is that your mother?" yes. "But she's a tea/
cher." Yes. I see that.) Reading, sunned, outside,
I see your lit hand on the page, spirea
Shaking light on us; from your ring I see slide
A sun, showering its planets across skies
Of words making, as you read or I or we,
A cosmos, ours. Its permanence still defies
The dark, in sparkles on this page; fiery,
It makes its statement clear: light multiplies.
No matter on whose flawed hand what jewel rides
Or who quickens to what bird with jeweled eyes,
The light of the planet is amplified.
Bird your life is diamond and amplifies.

REPLAY.

The luck beyond birds that was our quest
I find in you. Although I'm lost & late
Our hope at least lasted; here I still stand
In your dark love, efficient under day love;
It goes before me in the dark, its cries
Sharp. Wait, wait for me. Flash past, dusty bride,
Make your statement clear: light multiplies.

On the Country Sleep
of Susanne K. Langer

Though she lives there as the wood's
human creature, "carrying water,"
though in her sound shoes she is native to it,
the land even the boundary river

even when she sleeps
centers about her;
    centered it tenders
its myriad finalities
sunning them
in her energy of shaped ideas.

Focus of the forest focus
of the continent's intelligence
minded in the lucent
patience of her appetite
Susanne K. Langer doctor
thankless for wisdom's sake
entertains giant
ghosts, ours & her own; introduces
ideas to each other, reconciles
caves & skyscrapers of selves,
to become a familiar
of where the spirit lives
until even her sleep
is contemplative.

As beginning & end of that act she informs
her forest house.
To watch her in the high wood the night
is willing to be dark.
Beside her raised bed are pencils, yellow,
one in a mottled notebook keeping
her place. Between earth
and elsewhere,
wisewoman, sleeping,
she keeps her place.

Tabled on up-state cliff top
bedrock New York Susanne is lifted up

and though about her the moonlight were
just moonlight,

she lies generic inside
the steep hush of the grove,
earthwoman, offered as
a symptom of our health through
treecrowns & expanding atmosphere to
the skies.

In so focal a biography such sleep
recalls the cast of sacrifice.

Queens' Secrets: The Poems of Marie Ponsot

BY CYNTHIA MACDONALD

THE LANGUAGE of her poems depends on everyday words used in a predominantly conversational syntax:

> Have you traces of her? That she got lost
> I'd never guessed; but from what I hear now,
> You never quite received her, though we
> thought
> She knew more than the directions well
> And would get by, skilled in what not to ask.
> Were her efforts at lipstick any good?
> (Half-Life)

At first, the gleam and polish that distinguish a formal virtuoso seem absent. What is missing, perhaps, is that incantatory hum [see our interview of Ponsot] she wishes to banish; and the lack of it increases the sense that something almost haltingly everyday, rather than extraordinary, is taking place. At some point, though, we recognize that "Half-Life" is a sestina. Indeed, not content with an envoy that uses all six end words in their original order, Marie Ponsot adds a line and uses all six within it! So it is the very naturalness of her language, its lack of strain, that reveals the virtuoso's mastery of this form.

Ponsot's skill in crafted uses of forms includes villanelles, sonnets—virtually all traditional forms. Her mastery is phenomenal. The end of the sestina "Half-Life" deserves a mark of exclamation. "Late" deserves many exclamations for its beauty and naturalness within the restrictions of the coronel, that most bravura of forms in which the linking of stanzas and the intricate pattern of interlocking rhymes necessitate as many as nine employments of the same rhyme. Poem after poem, in fact, shows us the poet who grew up ingesting rhyming forms, making them a part of herself, then, in turn, making

them delectable for us. Moreover, as we can see in the last lines of "For a Divorce," she is able to transform mundane rhymes, the kind which are the end-stuff of pop songs, into resonantly expressive forms:

> exactly I do
> darkly I do
> recall the you of then when
> every time you touched me it was true.
>
> Deaths except for amoeba articulate
> life into lives, separate, named, new.
> Not all sworn faith dies. Ours did.
> (1) I am now what I now do
> (2) Then in me
> that stunning lover
> was you

The majority of Marie Ponsot's poems deal with biography, hers or those of others; and she maintains that the reader must have a specific sense of who the "I" in each poem is. Thus, the risk she takes, even in those poems utilizing characters distinct from the poet, is that her work may appear too self-focused, a kind of untransformed "This Is My Life." But it is a measure of her skill in her use of forms, the pulls of her various vocabularies and images, her metaphors employing nature, numbers, grammar, that the real life she depicts achieves the heightened life of fictiveness:

> To look from high places without flinching
> (I do it belly to the ground) is to suspect how
> speech
> might work, were we ready to face
> this drop
> into our inner space and find for mind

45

however awkwardly words and syntax
to negotiate aloud what otherwise
is mystery.

(Gliding)

Out of her lives, as a poet and, also, a bilingual translator, teacher, wife, mother, and, eventually, divorced woman, Marie Ponsot has become acutely conscious of partition and its burdens:

The pain of having two languages comes from a
straining between them in the mind,
from a need to further keep them separate and
a desire, forbidden, dangerous,
to marry them.

(Bilingual)

Parturition and partition; no wonder the poems deal with halves. In "Half-Life" there is the half-self lost by the choices made early in life, "beyond what I ask / lies the you you lost." In "Late," the other self is the mother, "half hidden, half disguised;" the poem begins and ends with an overriding sense of opposites, "two-poled" and "side by side." The opposition, bound always together as opposites must be, continues throughout: explicitly, as in "In the dark which is half of what words are made of," and implicitly, as in Ponsot's use of pairings—dark/bright and diamond/coal. When the self is the subject of a Ponsot poem, it is a divided self, with the parts bonded together—but uncomfortably so: sometimes complementary but, at other times, deeply conflictive. Sometimes, when she presents a self manifestly not her own, as in the poem about Susanne Langer, the parts are reconciled: Langer "introduces ideas to each other, reconciles / caves and skyscrapers of selves."

More often, however, reconciliation is not complete; there is a continuing struggle over what to keep and what to abandon in order to bond the divided self, yet distinguish its current self from its past self. This struggle appears in the fine poem, "Field of Vision: a map for a middle-aged woman." Here all three of Ponsot's most frequently traveled metaphorical roads (grammar, numbers, nature) are taken. "It is lonely (lone in likeness, singular, / Lovely (that is, like love)." As she describes waking alone in an apple orchard, the separateness which gives one identity as an individual must not only be

defined, it must be grammatically established and refined. Yet even with grammar's distinctions, separateness is not secure: "I feel perceived, perhaps as part of my perceiver." As another aspect of the one and the many, numbers are invoked: she counts pines, apple trees and other entities in the landscape and states there are six, "Three pairs. And? / and I / am her: / I name a / center a / point of view place." She must count, count herself, and notice that she is distinct from what surrounds her, including the sons and daughters, now grown: "I now disenchant the frozen totems of your names . . . . My ears . . . want a hush now and the new." This mother discovers her distinctness in reverse-telescope fashion from a baby who suddenly realizes he or she is not an actual part of the mother. Like the baby, the poet then embarks on a journey of discovery of separateness:

Though the woman walking is
Only me I am central among flashing
Differences (leaves like needles, leaves
That touch like fingers, leaves like islands,
The thousand ingenious ways of being green)

There is loss in what must be given up, the "fiery sugars" of "apples sweet with old storms," but there is also a sense of excitement in being "washed unstiff of history." A "Half-Life" is thoughts of life alone, without a better- or worse-half; it is life without the umbilical children; but it appears also as the new life explored in "Field of Vision": middle-age, the dark wood.

The poet-teacher-mother-divorced woman lives in Queens in her middle-age, the place where her seven children were born and the setting for the notebooks in which she accumulated poems and the pieces of poems. Although Marie Ponsot continued to write poems after her early book, *True Minds*, she rarely published them. It was not until her children were well on the way to independence, and after her divorce, that she re-emerged: "even the well-known secret witch must leave / her cave of shadows and come out / wearing a name it's safe to say aloud."

The title of her new book, *Admit Impediment* (Knopf, 1981), tells us a lot about Ponsot's vision of what the impediments to her career were. The allusion, also present in the title of her first book, *True Minds* (Pocket Poet series, City Lights, 1956), is to

Shakespeare's sonnet, 116, "Let me not to the marriage of true minds admit impediments." Ponsot's substitution of "impediment" for "impediments" is an illuminating change. Ponsot strongly suggests that a central cause for the division of true minds in marriage is caused by the expected enactment of the woman's role, as, "Most who expect nothing / for work well done / are women" (Sois Sage O Ma Douleur). If she is angry about the subjugation of women by men, she is equally angry that women have been taught to permit it. This is where Ponsot's angers swirl. Never about her children; she does not see them as impediments.

Affirming her role as mother, Ponsot recognizes that, if the pieces of poems which once filled the notebooks as the children grew are to come together, the magnetic attraction of the children, their "great power" over her, must now "evaporate." But how to allow this change, released from motherhood? She invokes magic rites (still not allowing an incantatory hum—"That's the thing I try to take out.") to effect the changes she wants:

> She thinks about helping, thinks
> Where to shop for the white rose,
> The white bird, in the proper places
> Sets saucers of water on the floor
> Of her Queens house.
>
> (Curandera)

In that house she becomes a monarch:

> I am magnificent, a tapestry
> Worthy, one of the Nine Beyond Jeopardy.
> My crown in gold thread forgives my face.
> Too late, I see I learned this pride of place.
> (Version of unfinished poem)

Of course, she worries that it is too late. But it is not, for she has already escorted the nine—husband, self and seven children—beyond jeopardy and has become ruler, not of the domestic domain but of the domain of art, the tapestry whose thread is made of words.

She has written a poem for Keats, and he wrote one which could have been for the Ponsot of earlier years:

> Blue! Gentle cousin of the forest green,
> Married to green in all the sweetest flowers—
> Forget-me-not—the bluebell,—and, that Queen
> of secrecy.

But Marie Ponsot is no longer the gentle Queen, living a life of secrecy in her appropriately named borough. In the poem "For John Keats, on the sense of his biography" she announces that, even though the risks can be acute, she has defied impediment and admitted speech:

> Full of blood or words his mouth
> lifted up the shape of the present tense.
> That present is the secret poets dare not keep
> or tell.   It makes them mind.   It makes them
>   speak.

For this we are thankful. Marie Ponsot's work is passionate, fierce and quiet, full of the authenticity and authority of years of writing and living, yet it is more than that. The poet's spirit lifts us up, moves us into the risk-filled realms—unfashionable realms—which are transcendent, full of wonder, even glorious.

CYNTHIA MACDONALD divides her time between New York City, her birthplace, and Houston, where she co-directs the creative writing program at the University of Houston. Her latest book of poems is *(W)holes* (Knopf, 1980). In the fifties and sixties she pursued a career as an operatic soprano before returning to school for an M.A. and a new career as writer and teacher.

Interview with Marie Ponsot

BY ROSEMARY DEEN

Question: If we began with the family, was there anything in your family that started you as a writer or sustained you?

MP: Those early experiences with language were somehow central. Certainly my family was a very verbal family. And they were storytellers, especially my father. My mother had a whole set of little tales she told me when I was very small. I remember being in the car one time and asking for a story. She picked up a book and started to read it to me, but I said, "No, no. I don't want that kind. I want the kind that's from your mouth."

Question: Even that sort of family doesn't always produce children who want to write the way you do.

MP: As far back as I remember I've always taken for granted writing is something you have to do all the time.

Question: Isn't that mysterious?

MP: Yes. I can't say how I learned very early that writing was an unfailing pleasure—sees you through times when there isn't anything you can do. You can't write anything that anyone else would want to read, but you can write just the same, for pleasure.

Question: Your family encouraged you?

MP: Oh, yes. My grandmother and mother both knew a lot of poems by heart. So I think it was natural for me to see poetry as the central part of literature. I knew that was where the real intensity came, the real excitement.

Question: Do you think your mother pushed you to write?

MP: Oh, no. My parents thought it was "nice" that I wrote. My poor mother, who had perfect Palmer method handwriting, used to try to get me to write to improve my wretched-looking handwriting. She would try to get me to make a clean copy for my father before he came home.

Question: How old were you when you began to write poetry?

MP: I don't remember not doing it. "Write poetry" is one way of saying it, but what I did usually turned out to be quatrains. Then I remember the time I had written something that I really thought was a poem, and it was so important to me that I hid it under the blotter inside my desk drawer. It was terribly exciting to me. I don't remember anything about it except its title, which was "Egotism." I suppose I had just discovered the word "egotism."

Question: What about the poems you sent to the *Brooklyn Eagle* lady, Aunt Jean? How old were you then?

MP: About 8. They were usually nature descriptions. I thought Nature, being quite important, belonged in poems. That's one of the nice things about having written when I was too young ever to think there was such a thing as a cliché. I remember writing about the "bloom" on a bunch of grapes. I didn't know what the word for that was. I asked my grandmother; she said that was the "bloom," and I thought that was wonderful.

One of the reasons I thought poetry was natural was that both my mother and grandmother not only knew poems but used to say the poems they knew by heart. There was no inhibition about speaking a poem. I remember going to the Brooklyn Botanical Garden and hearing, for perhaps the ten thousandth time, a poem my mother put me to sleep with many nights: "I Wandered Lonely As a Cloud" (the Garden has a magical hill of daffodils that used to do all those Wordsworthian things every spring). I remember more than once my grandmother, seeing the sun go down, said, "Sunset and evening star,/And one clear call for me."

Question: Where do you think you get a sense of the sacred? Of course you can't place the source of that in your early life, but . . . ?

MP: Yes, but I do remember it would be clearly exhibited by just stopping and looking at things. I can remember a field of daisies on Long Island somewhere. We had driven out to The Hamptons, and on the way back my mother said, "We don't really have time to stop." But then we came to a field of flowers and we stopped. It was a total field of daisies—I can still see it. Everyone got out of the car and just stood there, looking at the daisies in the late light of a summer's day. Not to pick a lot of them, but just to look at them. It is that kind of *stasis* or stopping, being stopped by a sense of what is sacred or beautiful or breathtaking.

Question: One of the things that students—that anyone wants to know is, How do you live your life? I don't mean the events of your life, of course, although you've had a pretty eventful life: an unfortunate marriage, and you've taken care of your seven children while earning the family living. But I mean your life as a writer. What were your priorities?

MP: Well, if you take an extreme example—take Lowell, it's easy to imagine that there was an assumption from the time he was small that the main thing in his life would be to make poems. And I can imagine that being true of many men who are talented in any direction—and of very

few women (of my generation). The thing that came first in a woman's life—and I think it should come first in everyone's life—is "Be good, sweet maid and let who will be clever." [from "A Farewell" by Charles Kingsley] The idea was that it would be accomplished in one of the conventional ways for women: you would be a wife and mother, or you would be some sort of socially helpful person. That would have priority over something like "being a great poet." I have never thought that I would stop writing poetry, not ever. I always thought that I would write poems, but I never thought they came first in my life, never thought that was my first obligation.

Question: What was your first obligation?

MP: Family. And—even now—how I earn my living, something I do in a very whole way—I teach. That has equal priority with writing poems. Fortunately, I find teaching very energizing. It's also very time consuming.

Question: Then how do you live your life as a poet? How do you write?

MP: Well, I like to have a notebook around that I feel comfortable with, a sewn notebook, a serious notebook with paper that is pleasing on both sides—nonsense like that. I re-write a good deal. I almost always start with a phrase. Sometimes that phrase doesn't survive—sometimes the poem takes it own way, but it's nice to have a notebook because you can write down such phrases and what comes along with them, and then not fuss with them—go back to them later and try to see the shapes of them.

Question: You once took it for granted that you would be writing in conventional forms?

MP: Yes, but by the time I was 14 or so I had discovered the permissions of free verse. For me at that point, a poem had to be incantatory. It had to be trying to move in the direction of magic. And that's the thing I try to take out now. That hum, you know.

Question: Did you see some of the directions poetry might go in when you were translating?

MP: You can see in La Fontaine that he creates a very special space in each of his poems because they offer such elegant shapes. You see that poetry makes you feel that its limits are the limits of a small world, but that the world is full. It was, in fact, in order to make that world, that I began using the first-person singular pronoun a lot, in a serious way. If the reader has no sense of who the "I"—the speaker of the poem—is, that space is harder to define.

I guess for me the biggest change was about 10 years ago. I wrote a poem about my divorce. And there were things in it that were not literally true to my own state. (I have never tried to write auto-biographical poems—it wasn't *that* I was worried about.) And truth became an issue for me and is now when I write. It has to be something that I call privately *true*. That has been useful to me because I think that I am rather an optimistically emotional person. I love grand visions. I love Easter when you say, *Haec Dies*, you know. And if you're not careful to say only what is true and not let emotion leak over to places where you don't really assign it to the words, then you get something bombastic.

Question: You had a pretty good apprenticeship in forms, I think.

MP: I did. Someone once said that what you should do is write a sonnet a day and that will make you a real poet. But there are so few instructions of-fered—no one tells you what to do next—so I took that quite seriously and literally and wrote a sonnet every day when I was about 20. They were pretty awful sonnets, but that didn't matter. I pushed them out to be sonnets, and they had to be completed by the end of the day. I didn't even try to make them serious—one was about cats' whiskers. But they had a conventional split, a conventional rhyme scheme, and ten syllables to the line. I think what that does is loosen you up, so that if you happen to have something that fits toward that shape, it's not impossible to do it. It's a greater freedom than not having that enlarge-ment. I think all conventions are intended to en-large your freedom and to bring things out of your mind that otherwise would get stuck in it.

Question: This was a time when that appetite for form you spoke of was active.

MP: Yes. After that, I began to try other things: vil-lanelles—you know, all the "mean" ones. And I began noticing what the form does to the work. Then the writing becomes difficult. You can no longer just write a poem about the cat.

Question: Did you have time to write other poems when you were writing a sonnet a day?

MP: Well, that's the thing. I think you can pretty safely say that if you're forcing yourself down the road of a convention, it's likely that you'll write other things that you want to write, as if in-spired—you know, the way some people imagine all poems are written?

Question: And you've done a lot of work translat-ing—that is another kind of apprenticeship. You told me once that in one stretch of 42 lines, La Fontaine uses only two rhymes. In fact, you've now had a lot of experience writing poems. Shall we say it?

MP: (whispers) Fifty years.

Question: If you could say something out of your own experience to a young writer or to a writer having difficulties, what would you say?

MP: I certainly would recommend that people not be afraid to try the conventions. Lots of practice of the conventions changes one's ear, amplifies the kind of thing one hears, and makes the writing of verse in the convention of free verse richer and more chosen, more personal. Writing quatrains and, when you get around to it, couplets, has got to free you from being unable.

Question: And you write every day?

MP: Yes, although there were years when that was not so. I think that is the most important thing I would say to anyone.

Question: What about "blocks"?

MP: I think that comes from misplaced attention. You can get blocked the minute you start thinking about yourself or the product. Prolific writing or non-stop writing—writing whatever comes into your head, not letting the pencil leave the page for 20 minutes—is one way to get around that. You're bound, in 20 minutes, to find some phrase that comes enough from the matrix of your real idea—not just the surface noises—so that you'll be able to work with it. And if, at that point, you think you still have nothing to do with that phrase, I would say, "Well, write a quatrain." At that point form will pluck out of the mind something good.

Question: You have done that?

MP: Sure. There have been times in the dark of the year, the pit of the semester, when life is very crowded with students' writings and impressions, and the wish to make sense out of what they are doing in some way that will be useful to them. It's hard then to take any time to write, but you can always write 20 minutes a day—those bits, non-stop. Of course that's not composition. But when summer comes or when Easter comes, some time comes. There's a little more light, a little more energy, and you have something to go back to. You're way ahead. The equipment is simple and the time requirement is simple—just have a pencil, a piece of paper, and what's inside you.

Question: When you sit down to do this prolific writing, do you have a word in mind, or do you really just start with the first word that comes to mind?

MP: Usually, when that's all I can do, I don't have much going for me but dogged determination. Sometimes, all I can write is *the*. I don't have anything to say, so I wait to see what noun is going to follow. It really is a question of keeping the door to your own language open.

Question: There are no rules?

MP: The equipment is simple and the time requirement is simple. You've got 20 minutes, and, say you do it for two weeks and you're only lucky twice. First, you made some record of what was available to you in your head on those days. Second, you've kept your subconscious working for you in the direction that says, "I want to write. I am a writer and I write, and I want to write what is true to me in what language my head holds for me."

And I think that in all areas of what we call original thinking, the preconscious life is a very active agent, if you ask it to be.

Layle Silbert

ROSEMARY DEEN has two passions (after her husband and five children): teaching and poetry. She studied poetry with John Arthos and Robert Lowell. Currently, she teaches at Queens College of New York, edits poetry for *Commonweal*, and writes poetry for herself. With Marie Ponsot, she is the author of a book on the teaching of writing.

Marie Ponsot: Biographical Notes

Marie Ponsot, daughter of William and Marie (Candee) Birmingham, had an early interest in language. There was some fostering of this within her home in a very natural way. Rosemary Deen, in notes to us about her interview with Ponsot, tells of Ponsot's mother's and grandmother's familiarity with poems,

the point being that they never quoted parts of poems as if from books—but, when they were stimulated by sights and the flow of conversation, they would simply *say* relevant pieces of poetry in an impromptu manner. [See our interview.]

Ponsot graduated from St. Joseph's College for

Women, in Brooklyn; she took her M.A. from Columbia the following year. Toward the end of the forties, she married Claude Ponsot, an artist who later became a professor. This turned out to be an unfortunate marriage and, later, they were divorced. In 1948–49 she did post-graduate work at the University of Paris. During and following that study she was a UNESCO archivist in Paris. She has lived in north Africa, and she still frequently travels, now often returning to France, where she recently spent sabbatical time.

The mother of one daughter and six sons, she always took much pleasure from the children, as well as from writing. Both provided her many daily joys. It has been said that Ponsot never stops writing. Friends have seen her write in a room full of people, even when the children were still small and playing all about the room. Often a child had to push aside her papers to climb on her lap—then push them aside to climb off again. Perfectly tranquil throughout these interruptions, she would simply pick up the words again.

She began a career in the writing field early, as Juvenile Production Manager for Crowell publishers. Also early, she worked as a translator and adaptor of children's classics—fables, tales, fairytales and other works. She translated from classic writers such as Charles Perrault, Grimm, and La Fontaine, well-known stories such as "Snow White" and "Cinderella." To give one example about Ponsot's productivity, in the decade between 1956 and 1966, seventeen of her books were issued. Her early poetry book, in an avant garde series by City Lights

(1956), was followed by many translations and adaptations for such publishers as Grosset, Golden Books, Signet, and Simon & Schuster. Her critical articles and reviews appeared in periodicals of the time and she received Gold Bell awards for writing the best religious radio program and the best television program (The Death of Judas). Following *True Minds*, she published little poetry for 25 years, yet won the Eunice Tietjens Memorial Award from *Poetry* in 1960; additionally, her poems were printed in other magazines and some were anthologized.

Russian Fairytales (1974) and *Chinese Fairytales* (1974) are now in print in her own name; under the pseudonym Michel-Aime Baudouy are *More Than Courage* (1966) and *Old One Toe* (1959); *Bemba: An African Adventure* (1966) appears under the pen name Andree Clair. In the mid-70s, she wrote a metrical translation of the 12th century Anglo-Norman poet Marie de France.

She teaches full time at Queens College of the City University of New York. She began years ago as a Lecturer in the SEEK (Search, Elevation, Education, Knowledge) program for underprivileged high school students; Ponsot currently teaches all phases of writing, including craft of poetry, poetry workshops, and introduction to editing. In addition, she broadcasts monthly hour-long programs for an NYC educational radio station, WBAI. On the air during the last four years, she has interviewed writers and also done reviews.

Knopf just released her new poetry book, *Admit Impediment*.

Celia Gilbert

CAMBRIDGE, MASSACHUSETTS

Alice Lyndon

The Stone Maiden

White butterflies settle on blue grass.
The stone maiden rises. Leaning
On black canes she balances,
Stiff-legged, to the pool's edge.
"Daddy?" Her heart
Pounds the length
Of her body,
Swelling breast and nipple
Under her crocheted bikini.
He pulls her in. He moves
His hands on the arch
Of her frozen back,
Trails her like kelp
In the tumbledown sky.

Pink petals fall on the wicker chair.
She whispers her wishes.
He shivers, close to that nakedness.
Her hands clutch at the air while he
Settles her at the table
And pours tea.
Oh my daughter what has been done to you?
Desire lies down in the wick.

At the Ball

Sad eyes, my owl, my groom
wearing your forked tails,
we cling, twirling and turning
away from a dark lady with silvery knees
and her partner, a holy man
tatooed with moons.

Carnival of teeth and tears.
Pell-mell of bodies. In the torn light
faces whirl above fluttering rags.
Waltzes surround us, move us
to pieces; the music pumps blood
through our hollows.

Beloved, outside the grass lies sleeping,
the stars flow through water,
but here, tapping his bossed wand
the dancing master, smiling,
beats the measure that
locks us in motion.

Joan Larkin

BROOKLYN, NEW YORK

Trudy Rosen

Sleeping on the Left Side

"I primaled it," she said
the smooth word like "marbled"
embarrassing me.

She remembered
being kept
from the camps—
she was three.
On that field at the edge
of death
her mother kissed her,
her father did not
look
up. Thirty years
later, the Dutch woman
said, "Yes, it did happen
that way
when I saved you."

"But what
about the side?
Did you wake me that year
so I wouldn't sleep
on my left side?"

"That side gives bad
dreams, they say,
and you had nightmares
every night—we had to turn you
over."

Her nightmares are over,
she tells me:
they rose to her

throat—she screamed—
she "primaled" them
away.

But for me, her dreams
are just beginning—
her mother's kiss—unfinished—
her father's bent head.

Cow's Skull with Calico Roses

Nothing soft in this skull
hung up, somewhere—
so it appears in this print
though to be painted
it must have been laid on cloths.
The black split between two continents
of white linen
could be O'Keeffe's table.

Sheets—softly folded
petals of flesh—
or abstraction:
white labia
or a white cello
fretted with thick silk stems
of a calico rose
concealing the cow's jawbone.

It's hard to see things
as they are said not to be,
but harder
not to see the cross
imposed on this flat sheet,
the split in this

tradition of painted space
she chooses.

She takes West to its limit
in this picture. Bleached
needlework flowers
hint of women's hands,
hot afternoons.
Hard not to see
the farmhouse, white
blister on the land.

Christ could be in this,
or the painter's faith
in desert light.

But I see an abortion—
papers torn to bits
with words on them—
a body fretted
by an unlike nature.

A disappearance, an abyss—
in this skull shaped like a pelvis
cracked in the center,
the black vertical plummeting
into a calico spiral,
the unlikely collaboration
of things to outlast a life:
its artifacts and bones.

Cynthia Macdonald

NEW YORK, NEW YORK

The Mosaic Hunchback

In the Hanging Gardens at Graz stands Grosswunch,
The Mosaic Hunchback, a twelve-foot marvel designed by
The visionary architect, Moses Wurmtaffel in 1520,
Executed, but never killed, by generations of Grazers,
Bit by bit. Part parti-colored completion, part empty
Filigree, each orifice—space defined by stopped space—
Accepted and accepts its new propitiation, bite by bite.

    The women say, "We have a Guild; the gold
    Sign in the shape of a pregnant belly hangs
    Outside the hall where we meet."
                Join us, join us.

As in the old tales of competition for the hand of
The maiden, marriages cannot be consummated until
The suitor finds his assigned piece—a shard of flesh-red
Feldspar from Peking, the tip of an orange goose-beak
From Hanover, a sliver of silver Electra wing from Seattle—
And has sealed it into its hole, its wet grout mouth.

    Each week on Monday the women meet
    To exchange words: faceted or rubbery or
    Covered with blood; words: quietly, softly
    From mouth to ear. We hear what we hear.
                Join us, join us.

Der Grosse Moses had set the task of keeping
The spirit alive to the whole town, piece by piece.
Men, it is said, do their part in action—the search—
And humped affirmation: "Peace in our town;
Embroider that on our festival banners," they order.

    They say women have only their tears—
    Running freely as salt, the cellar's

Mosaic bit, or water, its release—
And their parts which the men believe
They assign. But we know they do not.
                    Join us, join us.

The Hunchback had only one eye from 1810 until last week.
Now the shoemaker's son has put in the second—
The wood knot of a Blue Beech tree he went to Poland Springs
To find. Defined now, and defining, he claims his pride,
His bride, and smiles as they play Lohengrin, reminding her,
In spite of her beseeching, there can be no questions.

        Some women warn, "There are rules and rulers
        As sharply delineated as the side of one or
        The slide." Others say, "They wear clothes,
        But we see them naked, see their mosaic skin."
        "We, too, can have patterned flesh," say three,
        Standing on a Super Giant box of *All*. Some wring
        Their hands trying to decide; some know.
                    Join us, join us.

The Hunchback presides over the town's brocade ceremonies,
Looking on now with both eyes. It is said that two
Unmentionable holes must remain open, so that each Spring
The newly hatched maggots may pour out: to clean
The town's flesh, to leave the bones of the town polished,
To signify that the Holy Ghost resides where he will.

        Each week on Monday, the women meet.
        The shoemaker's son's wife comes, holding
        Her baby whose skin is as soft as
        Lamb's wool socks. The three women want
        To pick holes in it to form a mosaic baby.
        We expel them with plain skin and lullabies.
        Join us, join us.

When the holes run out, will they make a bride for him?
The mosaic Hunchbreast? Will the Hunchback design her or
Have designs on her? No one knows. The mosaic egg could be
Halfway around the world or it could contain the universe.
Blood myths are as hard to hold as blood. They cannot be read.

        Join us, join us.

Remains—Stratigraphy:

(for L.D.)

> must be used with caution for the altitude
> at which an object is found does not
> necessarily determine its stratum.
> Something that dropped into a well belongs
> not to the level where it was found at
> the bottom of the well, but to the level
> from which it had been dropped.
>   THE ANCIENT NEAR EAST

1979: Forty-nine inches in New York this year:
Melting, freezing, snow on ice, snow melting,
Freezing into ice, layers covering layers as
The Babylonians covered the Assyrians;
The Assyrians the Chaldeans; the Chaldeans
The Kassites; the Kassites the Amorites;
The Amorites the Sumerians. In the summer
Will we find fragments of the Ishtar Ziggurat
Or thick, brown Manhattan beads?

Ice, a frieze on buildings, forces everything
To stay where it is. Cars rock
Back and forth like women in labor,
Like women in labor needing Caesareans.
Their sound wakes us, interrupts our meals,
Stops our work, makes us bite our nails,
Causes attacks of migraine or colitis.
Some agony touches us even though we know
It is only a Firebird, a Grand Prix, a Lark.
I hold with those who claim someone dies
When tires fight ice.

The layers of your letters, sheets stained blue,
Pile into a bed. Endearments, promises, lies

Twist like a wet handkerchief.
1973: You wrote of spring wasps outside your
        window,
That the fiery nails of their sting . . .
On the Anacassia Savannah Plain
The Carmine Bee Eater rides the Bustard to
Catch bees or locusts which the Bustard's large
Fringed wings comb from the brush. In locust years
Cicadas fall in blizzards on the Bustards.
The Bee Eater rides and eats
Using its carmine beak to warn its mount of danger.

1975: You wrote of the tattooed man,
His skin like paper, water-marked with patterns:
Aphrodite drowning in the vortex of his navel,
Diana wrinkled until passion made her
Spring smooth . . .
On the High Simian Plain
The Gelada Baboon flicks its long silky hair
Against flies. It woos by combing hair with its nails,
Picking fleas, licking secretions clean.
Wooing by grooming, the overlord
Turns his pink rump to his harem's chosen one.
You wrote, hear me, believe me:
These letters spell messages as compact and
        complicated
As a tattoo of passion's fingerprints.

1979: Taps.
Music of ice cascades to the pavement.
You write: I hope you are well.
Nails of ice puncture water, merging with it;
A stratum cannot be assigned.
Reflections of stone tattoo the surface.
Whatever the object was,
Nothing remains.

Toi Derricotte

ESSEX FELLS, NEW JERSEY

Layle Silbert

The Testimony of Sister Maureen

Sister Maureen Murphy, a teaching nun in
the Rochester-based Sisters of St. Joseph,
was arraigned in June, 1976, on a charge
of first-degree manslaughter in the death
of her newborn son. In 1977, she was tried
and declared "not guilty."

> I know it matters if I'm convicted, but
> I've already imprisoned myself in my mind
> and heart. I'm imprisoned because I can't
> escape from my thoughts. I want to know if
> I harmed the child. I know I must have, because
> I was the only one there.
> > From a conversation with psychiatrist
> > William Liberston on May 20, 1976.

I

        she enters the convent . . .

A woman leads me in,
red tiles and clerestory windows,
the sun bleeds in like beets;
"My daughter," she says
not kindly nor unkindly, but as if
her tongue were tied in her head
and hooked like a deformity to her smile,
"Sell your lover's heart for Christ."

    We eat the blood-soaked
    stone,
        dislodge
    thigh,
        crack
    dry skin in our teeth,

as if the grit of innocence must
match the muscle in our jaws.

II

My skin grows black.
I burn.
My eyes pale like lepers.
I wear goat-fur, stink of sin
in the middle of their kindness.
Under my hood,
I do not pray as they think—
my eye turns pink with rage
clear as the nucleus of germ.
These are the works of God:
The miracle ignites Him in my bones.

III

The children in my care
with wisp-thin wings
like butterflies of glass
fly to the brown
floor of my shuttered room,
their music in my book
like a rush of wet sweet air.
I come down to meet them,
breathing in the iron
corset,
head,
      spinning
    loose and fragile,

floats like an angel in a starched white pinafore;

I rush with arms
to shut the gap.

Fit airless bodies
in this chewed
                    curve of my spine

IV
a man comes in the bar,
        this is a dream, it seems
        to be a dream
        how did i get
        in this seaport town, how
        did i trawl
        this black lobster
        with my own hand
        how did i latch
        him by the throat
        & hand him my life
        my penny, bravely

i drink a beer,
the glass slick in my hand
as sea; the room
smells of fog & night
myself, in a black cotton dress
the table top, unwashed
blurred as a drunk man's face

(where are my sisters
like bells they are
shivering in that dark tower)

he follows me,
a presence in the bushes
like an image in a black mirror

the moon breaks.
                    his face
                    is ashes
in the crowns of trees

V
        the air hums at night
        the wings of bees
        beg for entrance at my ears
        return to the familiar nest
        it is spring
        this year there is a heart
        at its center
        red with thorns

He grinds me muscle thick
i cannot shut the singing out

VI
one night   i place my ear
against the wall

                            sometimes
i hear Him
out there
                    sometimes
i feel Him

shake the floor
lonely as a devil.
                                    i
drive through darkness
in harness
                    look
not left
nor right
for fear
            His eye,
                lidless & white,
watches
                            tonight
            i hear
no one,
        but
blood
seems
singing out of veins,
                                    veins
cracking in the
center of the
plaster
till
all the halls
                        are white

            i
            have touched
            pain
            laid my hand
            on it
            & felt it
            climb like mountains
            in the air,

       tonight
this
Demon
      tears
dark
   out of the sky

    i/
      rise

       i/
part

    like skin

over

His goat heart

VII
the child is dead.
they bring him in a white boat
          to my bed
   like moses
   like the jew-child

i place him in the reeds
thickly hidden
in the salamander green
         and the brown bark

my stocking is around his neck

i am the maiden in the window
who watched him through the first

       bright

   ball of air,

       triumphant
       as a god,
          i am

god-
   mother,
        God
will take my place.

Yvonne

NEW YORK, NEW YORK

The Tearing of the Skin

I

All white
the boards, the shutters
a long shrill schoolteacher throat
is Aunt Ida's house
shouting up and down
the dirt brown neck of Brunswick Avenue
"I pledge allegiance"
straight up to the stark electric hair

of sudden rain.
Sudden white
is Aunt Ida's house
like the silk lining of dreams
we women of color learn to hide
porcelain flame
mandala pearl
but not our flag of surrender riding

riding the night like a tattered star
into the grey drowned hair
of a silent morning.
We women of color learn to brush away
water of a harpsichord
like lint from a husband's suit.
But Aunt Ida slipped
out of the scream she could not pull

(and it would not rot)
into her smooth strong bone
of a house, her good dry lace
hugging the front porch windows.
And after dark her twenty-five pale
window shades seem to uncurl

whatever sleeps.
And each ruffled organdy curtain

like an antebellum skirt
is light diverting cream
to bring in the cat.
And why not?
"If you work for less,
you won't get more."
Each room is a sedative
a cup of camomile tea.

Each room is a key.
Some are like vellum and some,
prim as soap. Each room
is a view. Far within
her old incurability calls "not pretty not
pretty" like an unrequited love.
And Aunt Ida replies "not at home
not at home" and begins her work.

Her work is to bury (if not
heal) the beggar in herself
to rebuild the altar, the foreplay
the white corset melting like wax.
Pale as a fingernail
her carpets open their thighs
the shorn and the shepherd alike
gathered in the wool.

And who will condemn?
The hungry? The one who is eaten?
Each is tight-lipped
about such wisdom
(because the paws of marriage
are permitted to sweat).

Each chair and spoon and sheet
is an act of aggression.

Let the icebox purr.
Her first anniversary plates
aspirin white
are heavy as skulls
(because the famine is always with us).
The sink and cupboard are wise.
The stove is puritan white
with hot blue paws. Yes,

every whatnot is costing
less than disaster.
Less than opium, self-pity, the first white
song of the apple.
This first white sugar
of a house. White bread. White shoulder.
Her brazen back
to the world.

II

Lorenzo swallowed his hot water and lemon
as if it hurt. Ida put two poached eggs
beside the once-a-week butterfish
with a touch of helplessness.
"A three-mile jog on an empty gut
would kill a bull," she said.
"Lucky for you,
I'm just a Negro man." And he was out

into the dawn white as his enemy
        into the cold
                succulent
                        mist
    he was amber   cougar   copper   gold
        his moccasin thighs
        pungent and hard
            and on the gravel
            glistening unfermented black
            his unbroken hooves
                    he disappeared
                    muscular glint
                    mercurial dust
                    what neither of them could
                        hold
                    astringent   electric
                    he was the salt ethereal

that never melts
he disappeared
don't love him to death
yet she lingered
before the narrow and steamy kitchen window
her whole life
pushed against the dawn
and the value of her face
without rouge or standardization
without make-believe or anesthetic
was indelibly black
unmitigated and mature
a blackness so elegant and sovereign and pure
yet he would never think of her
as lily or ladyslipper or rose

yet he would often call her
as if he were not lonely and molested
at any shadow of the week
in any freedom of the house
into his red impeccable dance
but she always refused
despite her loving it more
than the way he loved
the way he danced
like a soldier, a pugilist
of fire
muscular, glamorous, rhetorical
disciplined yet savage
labyrinthine yet geometric yet
reckless, witty, unpredictable, unpremeditated
yet conscious, too conscious
of an audience, the precision and the threat
of her need, her eyes
which were never envious
but always and almost irritatingly
appreciative, distilled
of all her desire beyond that of
the visual
every movement, gesture of him caressed
her love was like a magnet
refusing to hold.

III

            nobody's blind
            they said they said
            over your
            brazen puritan

hill robbing a
young sly delirium
your impeccable
flesh but not your
face they give it a
withering cradle year
you ought to be 50
ought to be
sucked out not
seven days a week
not five years
maneuvering
playing with
his vanishing fire
they said they said
you ought to be whipped

Ida thrusts
into her beauty parlor lock
three sober keys
her foot stabs the dark
no alarm
but a sudden chill
over her left shoulder
"I hope I don't need . . ."
somebody's whore
shivering
at 8:45

"I hope I don't need . . ."
"I've got nobody til 10.
Wash, press and curl?"
Perhaps Ida yawns.
Perhaps the customer giggles.
"How on earth how on earth
did you guess?
I want bangs
like Claudette Colbert—"
(only then does Ida perceive
the scar.)

Her crooked
female
scar
like a varicose
vein thick
common as the
common

why even the deacon's
in the middle of a
blizzard   dared
show her mimicry
of a marriage/face
so bruised so soft
yet so Hollywood
foolish dark
glasses never could
her Woolworth pearls
her rhinestone rot
he'd knock out of her
knock out of her

like a husband stick
Bangs like Claudette
Colbert   poodle
cut   pony
tail   a pirate
patch of hair
over the eye
as if glued
like Veronica Lake
but nobody's blind
nobody's blind

IV
Owlish, warty
prickly of speech
the barbed untouchable coat
of September chestnuts
Miss Clementine Hawks
every Thursday at noon
hobbled into the shop
interrupted Ida's lunch
and demanded
glorification.

Why couldn't she (hadn't she)
give it all away, all away
her chestnuts in late November
crazy with fermentation
the mulched wine
of those unchosen, untouched
in the wet forgotten undergrowth
of fallen leaves
monkshood
and wild mushrooms?

"Brew sage, Ida gal, or grapevine root
and when it's hot as curry, let it steep
'bout thirty minutes, then drench the hair.
It ain't holy for no young woman
to be grey. And if you got
trouble with snarls, put
oil of rosemary on the brush.
And if you got trouble with dandruff
take vinegar and mint, each a half
a cup with a cup of water
boil it, strain it, rub it hard
hard into the scalp.
And if you got trouble, I mean hell,
with your monthly, fennel tea
or red raspberry leaf
is best, and dill
if your mother's milk is stubborn
and marigold if your nipples are sore
and for migraine, drink camomile
and—what? palpitations of the heart?
Why roses, gal, roses never fail."

Yes, Clementine was everybody's
grandmother, now.
Everybody's tea, poultice,
spell against worms
and the croup.
Gnarled, indomitable,
sacred as the sassafras root
she exchanged
for an hour of grace
in Ida's hands.

Yes, she was everybody's
gypsy, seeress, nun
unapologetic and unshaken
windswept bone
like mountain juniper
such cleaving to an older truth
yet wasted, uprooted (somewhat)
like the twisted
precision
of random lightning.

V

Good Friday. Half-past three.
Aunt Ida's hairdressing parlor
was steamy and tight.

Early shadows crept.
It was spring on c.p. time.
Her *Jesus Saves*
hung like silver, bloodless
in those shadows,
where the squat jars and pearly bottles
cluttered the appointment desk,
where holy palms
adorned the strong cash register.

Oh, my young long soft wool hair
sweet lime
and yellow liquids mingle and foam.
Aunt Ida's fingers were cold,
brisk
her palms like the skin of mummies
dark
from years of perfumed oil
on hot comb handles.

A burly man entered
grandfatherly
a numbers runner.
Under the whirring dryer
under the wild wet hair
under the blind professional scratch
of Aunt Ida's brush
I shut my eyes
and heard the good women all around
sigh and giggle.
They were young and unashamed
their husbands home.

But soon he was gone.
And my ugliness was gone.
Washed, slicked, and furled
my feather curls tickled and teased
the haphazard eyebrows of childhood.
Yes. Beauty was truth.
And truth was always
on its way.
Jesus will rise.

VI

Radiant
glorified
effervescent
they scatter from beneath Aunt Ida's hands

the Negro women of this shambling town
a shattering of raven wings
chatoyant
falling
stars

Sinuous
pungent
smoke
is the everyday tumult in their eyes
desire, revulsion—even the street corner
women learn to spin
such ironic

diluted
threads

Such thwarted
succulent
fruit
cursed as toxic, unredemptive, impenetrable
side of the mirror (the black)
every day Aunt Ida touched
with such
clairvoyance
in her hands

Kinereth Gensler

BELMONT, MASSACHUSETTS

The Border

> The war broke out in autumn at the empty border
> between sweet grapes and oranges.
> YEHUDA AMICHAI

War or peace, the border is never empty,
growing its wildflowers and weeds,
making the most of a difficult position.

And the cash crops aren't meant for your table.
You're an old hand dragging that wagon to market:
grapes, oranges, wheat—

whatever the harvest, it's earmarked for export.
You ship it abroad, make do
with dandelion greens and milkweed.

When war breaks out,
weeds will sustain you.
You rely on chicory.
And the Good Soldier Thistle . . .

This story belonged to your mother,
it's the one she loved telling:

How at nightfall, after the first World War, in those
months of upheaval, stranded with a broken-down car in the
hills of Judea, afraid of the isolate terrain, afraid of
the driver, she saw from the road's edge a blue flower,
followed it into a stony field, and picked it.

In the fading light it was a beacon, blue as amulets
are blue. Reaching through thorns, her fingers uncovered a
box and wires, and a voice came to her out of the ground:
What number are you calling? May I help you?

After a time she answered, forcing herself to speak
into a field telephone, left over from the war, still
connected. She told what landmarks she had seen nearby,
where she had come from and where she was headed.

And rescue came. They lifted the car and driver
into a huge lorry, scooping her up, taking her straight
to her destination!

From her fear a woman makes a story
and tells it to her daughters.
Telling it, she names it:
The Blue Thistle.

In the blue blaze of thorn along the border,
in the desolate spaces,
a real voice speaks from the ground,
a weed called by its name becomes a flower.

Something brave is growing.

Marge Piercy

WELLFLEET, MASSACHUSETTS

Robert Turney

Shadows of the Burning

Oak burns steady and hot and long
and fires of oak are traditional tonight
but we light a fire of pitch pine
which burns well enough in the salt wind
whistling while ragged flames lick the dark
casting our shadows high as the dunes.

Come into the fire and catch,
come in, come in. Fire that burns
and leaves entire, the silver flame
of the moon, trembling mercury laying
on the waves a highway to the abyss,
the full roaring furnace of the sun at zenith
of the year and potency, midsummer's eve.

Come dance in the fire, come in.
This is the briefest night and just
under the ocean the fires of the sun
roll toward us. Already your skin is dark,
already your wiry curls are tipped with gold
and my black hair begins to redden.

How often I have leapt into that fire,
how often burned like a torch, my hair
streaming sparks, and wakened to weep
ashes. I have said, love is a downer we take,
love is a habit like smoking cancerous cigarettes,
love is a bastard art. Instead of painting
or composing, we compose a beloved.
When you love for a living, I have said,
you're doomed to early retirement without benefits.

For women have died and worms have eaten them
and just for love. Love of the wrong man or

the right. Death from abortion, from the first
child or the eighteenth, death at the stake
for loving a woman or freedom or the wrong
deity. Death at the open end of a gun
from a jealous man, a vengeful man,
Othello's fingers, Henry's ax.

It is romance I loathe, the swooning moon
of June which croons to the tune of every goon.
Venus on the half shell without the reek
of seaweed preferred to Artemis of the rows
of breasts like a sow and the bow
ready in her hand that kills and the herbs
that save in childbirth.

Ah, my name hung once like a can
on an ink-stained girl blue as skim milk
lumpy with elbows, spiky with scruples,
who knelt in a tower raised of Shelley's bones
praying my demon lover asceticism
to grant one icy vision.

I found my body in the arms of lovers
and woke in the flesh alive, astounded
like a corpse sitting up in a judgment
day painting. My own five hound senses
turned on me, chased me, tore me
head from trunk. Thumb and liver
and jaw on the bloody hillside
twanged like frogs in the night I am alive!

A succession of lovers like a committee
of Congress in slow motion put me back
together, a thumb under my ear, the ear
in an armpit, the head sprouting feet.
Kaleidoscope where glass sparks pierced

my eyes, in love's funhouse I was hung
a mirror of flesh reflecting flaccid ideas
of men scouting their mothers through my womb,
a labyrinth of years in other
people's thoroughly furnished rooms.

I built myself like a house a poor family
puts up in the country: first the foundation
under a tarred flat roof like a dugout,
then the well in the spring and you get
electricity connected and maybe the next
fall you seal in two rooms and add some
plumbing but all the time you're living
there constructing your way out of a slum.
Yet for whom is this built if not to be shared
with the quick steps and low voice of love?

I cherish friendship and loving that starts
in liking but the body is the church
where I praise and bless and am blessed,
singing the song that goes past words.
My strength and my weakness are twins
in the same womb, mirrored dancers under
water, the dark and light side of the moon.
I know how truly my seasons have turned
hot and cold around the lion-bodied sun.

Come step into the fire, come in,
come in, dance in the flames of the festival
of the strongest sun at the mountain top
of the year when the wheel starts down.
Dance through me as I through you.
Here in the heart of fire in the caves
of the ancient body we are aligned
with the stars wheeling, the midges swarming
in the humid air like a nebula, with the clams
who drink the tide and the heartwood clock
of the oak and the astronomical clock
in the blood thundering through the great heart
of the albatross. Our cells are burning
each a little furnace powered by the sun
and the moon pulls the sea of our blood.
This night the sun and the moon
and you and I dance in the fire of which
we are the logs, the matches and the flames.

Night Fight

Yin and yang, they say,
female and male but the real
division at the roots
of the world's knotty tree
is between those whom trouble
sucks to sleep and those
whom trouble racks awake.

In beds, narrow, double and king,
in matrimonial hammocks, on rugs,
in tents and sleeping bags they lie.
They have just quarreled. The rent
is three months overdue. The roof
leaks blood. The operation looms.
She stares at the ceiling
where demon faces flicker grinning
and he snores.

Suppose anger grips her,
a rat in a terrier's jaws.
How can you sleep?
she roars and he moans
How can you wake me?
groping for the clock.
It's three bloody a.m.!
Rolls over, diving.

He is a pumpkin ripening.
He is a watermelon of sweet
seedy dreams. He is a cask
seething with fermentation.
He bubbles like a hot spring.
He sticks to the sheets like mud.

Divorce or strangulation
is imminent. Those anxiety
stirs hate those anxiety
stills. The conscious
being conscious at four a.m.
cannot forgive.

Jane Augustine

NEW YORK, NEW YORK

Ray Ellis

After Yeats

I

Take care, he said, your poems are almost
too beautiful—he who used to make much
of my beauty. Under lovely images pain is lost
or blunted; do you want that? he asked.
                                  I'm tough,
I think, and unromantic, sworn to accost
my self-deception, but I'm re-reading Yeats and love
his elegance. I want to bypass pain and sing
my desert world in music golden and piercing.

II

Under noon sun she rides the white mare
down from the mountain, through boulders and
       pine.
She's wearing jeans and a green halter, with bare
brown back and shoulders, midriff lean
from pitching hay. Her hat falls back and frees her
       hair.
Her lover, who's dismounted, watches her. Two men
walk to her stirrup, offer up a coffee-can
of wild raspberries. She scoops a handful,

raises it red and dripping till the juice
runs down her arm. Slowly she licks
the fruit-blood off her skin. Her hair blows into
her mouth. Red smears her lips.
Throned in the saddle she sits sensuously
eating, and the men look down, abashed by it.
The horse stands and shakes the loose reins
while rubies splash onto her snowy mane.

I Help My Mother Move Out of Her Old House in the Country

I

It is not my life
under these lichened oaks,
      these redwood eaves
but my mother's life—

I was ten and climbed
a young laurel where she could
      not see me, and laurel leaves
touched my hair with pungent fingers—

She called and I came
back, and didn't mess up
      paper with my writing—
I followed her housework

inside stone walls.
Outside the rich stink of sun
      on grass and poison oak—
sleeping nights under unfinished

eaves, I covered my head
as a bat's wing
      fanned me in the dark

II

The house is a body
      from which we come;
now it is emptying out

Is it her life only
    that disappears as I am
packing, filing, discarding?

My mother sits in the bath
    massaging cramped legs,
in place of her right breast

the skin   pinned neat and flat
    across, under it the heart
pulsing.

In the pale water,
    slightly distorted,
her ankles, blue with burst veins

are slender as mine

III
Paintings done when I was 18, 22
    —mementos of talent
no room for these in

my make-shift apartment
nor for my father's *Schubertlieder*

but I take these: *vom Wasser*
    haben wir's gelernt
how to move on—
    maybe I'll sing yet.
Rain falls these nights

in dusty California. I sit up
    late and listen to the dripping.
Old papers in the garage await
    our junkman.
In the morning my mother

greets me in her green suit.
    Buds tip the laurels.
I wrap and mail to myself
    her old evening gowns.

We will never leave this place.

Kathleen Spivack

WATERTOWN, MASSACHUSETTS

Pam Mesker White

Humanitarian

it isn't as easy as you think
five daughters by a former marriage:
the new wife wants a son
the ex-wife attempts suicide
the oldest girl tries suicide
the second chooses drugs

the third has run away from home
the fourth's in boarding school
the ex-wife attempts pottery
then she does yoga: he pays the bills
and puts them all through therapy
the ex-wife gets depressed

he takes on more patients, lavishing
his love, his greatest earnings
he sees the first "case" at seven a.m.
the first wife tries to get a job
the second wife has quit her job
deciding she is barren

it takes a certain style of life
to support so much drama
he raises his fees, sees more neurotics
and sells off half the furniture
his new wife seeks encounter groups
to find why she fears childbirth

the oldest daughter gets knocked-up
he pays for her abortion
the ex-wife takes a lover but
she cannot keep the man
the second wife weeps in his bed
he turns over, he tries to sleep

one daughter flunks her final year
he sends her off to summer school
the second wife cooks dinner while
the ex-wife calls him up
she's incoherent, she drinks too much—
if only she'd get married—

when he hangs up, the food is cold
the second wife smiles, virtuous
his youngest girl's a shoplifter
he takes more private patients
all day there's crying in his ears
his brain's a telephone exchange

his daughters, cash, ring in and out
the ex-wife threatens suicide
he puts her pain in the register
the second wife takes pills
his patients, improving, sit and smile
as he makes exact change

Ntozake Shange

NEW YORK, NEW YORK

jonestown or the disco

shall we go to jonestown or the disco
i cd wear red sequins or a burlap bag
maybe it doesnt matter
paradise is fulla surprises
& the floor of the disco changes colors/
like special species of vipers/
no real musicians appear after 2:00 there is no dining
out/ shout hallalujah/ praise the lord

but shall i go to jonestown or the disco
if jesus wont fix it/ the deejay will
my step is off or on
my arms are sweatin in the spotlights twirlin or the sun
pick those tomatoes/ & join us in prayer
a tango might excite the crowd
a bolero give us salvation
freak freak freak
maybe i shd really consider the blue silk
every one at the office is looking for me on tv
tonite/ if i win i might die/ jesus help me
the kingdom comes
god moves in mysterious ways & koolaid is all we cd handle
even my aunt promised not to miss us
our children will be so proud/ gd dancers are gd lovers

but shall i go to jonestown or the disco
good lovers get married/ god shares the covenant
of marriage/ & marriage is the dance of life/ oh
we get so happy/ we so happy it's sin & we might die
thank-you jesus
god loves bringing wealth from the wilderness
yes lord
at the disco we shout the praises of the almighty
i wrap my arms around you till the end

are you ready/ are you ready to/ freak
we came here to feel good
thank-you jesus
to give joy & form to the world/ thank-you jesus
we came here/ yes lord
in our desire/ in hairshirts & satin
yes/ oh the power & the glory
amylnitrate/ makes you wanna die/ or dance yrself to death
why go to jonestown/ amen/ i say why go to jonestown
yes lord/ i'ma go to the disco/ where i cd dance myself to
death
shout hallalujah/ praise the lord

Lois Elaine Griffith

BROOKLYN, NEW YORK

For All the Homesick Sunshine Girls in Spring

And the new space she find was an antique
that drew she back to a root of simplification and definitions of love
in an expression of dream line water fingers
tracing designs in the sands of the home place
where she last kiss his face.
And yonder so dawn cracking,
hey, but look a nigh
from way far creeping up.
Now sunshine girl coming out
blooming out in fineries of lace and sashiness
all swishy-swishy and air-ified
like the sea foam that land she on these pavement shores.
But hey, Enid,
child, when last you see Lena Lime?
I na seen na heard from she since—
she running crazy in Port-a-Prince back from abroad and the States, yes,
after the fast life, miss.
But you know what me Granny say,
what go round come back again
and she be back home soon enough eating crow.
(Chups, tsk)
Child, I can't be bother me with people like that, sometime-y, sometime-y.
I never know she rest a moment,
always eager and anxious for a new turn.
And finally she finding out
that backward and foreso is the same place as now.
Yes, a woman such as she
having strange eyes to look upon what be foreign sights
and trails of laughter searching out for love
and loving ways and lovely movements deep inside
that is she, island lass ain't too fussy about the spring up here,
you know, a taste of honey worse than none at all,
changing up quick, quick, too short and fast a moment
all swishy-swishy and air-ified
like the sea foam that land she on these pavement shores.

Fire Wind's Song to Sundae (Loba)

She
wolf
carries a prairie story
when her grandmother's mother
made circle trails
silent new moons
the memory passed to her daughter's sensations
hostile to vermin like desert flies looking
        for a home.
She
wolf
carries a prairie story in her breast
under covered skies
she nurses her cubs
ancient mystery of what grows
hidden in mother's winter den
scour the forests for star dung
follow the scent of wounded warrior's blood.
The medicine mountain lies to the north.
The rains there are frequent.
The danger is starvation before spring.
A day's work is belly hunt.
The earth will eat her children
who cannot hold to her back.
She will make new children of their flesh.
She
wolf
carries a prairie story in her eyes
watching many sunsets
her dance is a journey
marking changing wind's howl in moon embers.

Celia Watson Strome

NEW YORK, NEW YORK

Nr. 6

"Want a boat?" ask God.
He lookin
just past me, an on upriver.

I nod, an look
way down river.
Empty water.
The light come back pewter.
Further down, on shore,
somethin white move.
I can't see what
thru scruff bushes.
It come an go in
small, disjointed rhythms.

"Git in then." God
sit back down
in the boat like wood,
sloped blue shoulders,
cocked head.

The boat barely rock
as I drop, my feet
roll soundless on the boat-thwarts.

God glance up, his pale eyes
gone pewter. He nods
to me, unfold his
thick hands against the oars.
The boat slip out.

I look back,
down the river, once,
to the shore.

It was a woman in white,
takin in the clothes.

Nr. 10

Thru fat crowds
her face ketch de light.

I sees her skin
foldin in an out a long wrinkles,
her eyes like ol
grey coats, shinin fron under
de lids.

She draw me
past snatches a flesh like
thru a woods, like cracked bracken
sprung aginst my chest,
I comes to her.

She begin to sing
fron out a de darkness
that curl itself like a
russle round de light

she sing, her thick mouth
one dusty star stuck in flesh.

When I gives her a dime,
she call on God t' blessin me.
I feel God's dry white breaths
meet mine, breath fer breath,
an rattle in my head throwed back.

Against de buildin, death,
lollin wit impertinent hands,

78

brush de head a de blind woman oncte,
an is gone.

I hurries on.

Nr. 12

"*Wake up!*" sez God.

I turn, mutterin
in the dark, bed-sheets
twisted under my feet.

A shudder roll through my house.

"The dam!" I leaps
from the matted bed, I rushes
to the street.

Naked bodies, pajama-bottom people,
all rushes in the street, wailin.
The dam stand
to the east,
blacker'n Jonas-spit. It pop
an groan all down the valley.

We turns an run,
soft feet slappin
the valley road, thousands
of night feet,
gruntin breath.

I shoots a look back. One long
gash come across it, silver.

I swings, stumblin at the sight.

The groanin, the pantin
grow still.
The dam, it crumble down
like dust.

An a terrible blindin
light roll down, soundless,
or filled wit mutterins
word-shavins,
bits of ol wood, worms,
like the tarnish come loose from its star,

like mem'ries, wore loose fron de night.

Nr. 19

I said to my mother,
"What have you done wit God?"

An she said,
"God? We put 'im
out in the back field,
cause every time people
come around, they stare at 'im,
an he was beginnin to act peculiar."

An I go out
to the back field,
work next to God,
shuck corn, corn silk
blowing down the row.

Phyllis Janowitz

ITHACA, NEW YORK

Mrs. Lucky

I have reached the right age. Speeding
adrenal molecules no longer skid
through my veins wearing crash helmets

and goggles like Mario Andretti.
Now they go in for a beer; they walk.
Or they take the local, hanging onto

a strap, reading *People* magazine
through bifocals. They forget to get
off at their stop. For whole hours,

maybe days, I am able to reassure
the young when their faces turn
blue with tears. Mick Jagger.

Mercedes Benzes. Gucci, Pucci.
Who cares? Whatever we get we
keep such a short time it doesn't

matter. I say this over. Often
pebbles are left in the sifter.
I'm old enough to stop such playing.

What can I buy with pebbles?
Another pint of blood? Once
our heads barely reached the sill,

the candy machine turned and turned,

heavy and slow: pink blue green—
hard lumps to suck but ocean sweet

as long as the last sticky pieces
stuck to our teeth. Now the flowers
darken and dry in their clear flask—

the legacy of summer. Sores won't
heal anymore. Something wants to cut
loose; something is trying to tear.

Anyone can see through me, hear
the liquids filter through my veins.
Muddy gravy. Tin can jello.

Overheated radiators, spitting blood.
Oh cold kiss approaching, sweeter than
any I've ever had, your breath smells

like the milk of my mother! Cheer-
leaders should chant elegies outside
my window. Give me a D, give me a D,

give me a D D D! I live on credit
in my final cell and it isn't good.
One gets used to bruised veins but not

the bills, or those hospital religiosos
steeped in recycled words, equating
indifference with the will of God.

Judith McDaniel

ARGYLE, NEW YORK

When Mother Died, Rows of Cans

When mother died, rows of cans
lined her basement shelves, defense
against impermanence, bought

when she was well. Not in fear
but thriftiness, she stocked
nineteen cans of grapefruit juice,

seven dill pickles and four
bottles of ketchup marked
a nickel off. Her jarred

preserves, magenta beets, stood
in rows three deep. For two years
before she died, she had not left

her bed. We threw away small
personal things—her glasses, jars
of cream—but could not touch

those basement shelves, abstractions
honed to artifact, her voice
and hand, memory of her touch.

Snow in April

At noon you call
Feed the birds
you tell me robins

are starving they've
no place to land
and their food all
under the snow.

I carry out
the last scoop of sun-
flower seed, scatter
robinfood in the mud
tracks your car left
this morning and wade
back through ankle
deep snow while robins
hop awkwardly from low
branch to low branch.

Jacketless in April
sun I split two logs
at the woodpile. Squint-
ing at the too blue sky
one random cloud
a hawk's white coasting
belly circling sky high
watching for a hint
of red breast down
on the muddy road.

From my window I watch
robin's nervous hops
come to rest. She
wades her tired feet
in mud and pecks
at last summer's
final seed.

June Jordan

NEW YORK, NEW YORK

Lynda Koolish

This Is a Poem about Vieques, Puerto Rico

Vieques is a tiny island about half an hour
by prop plane from San Juan.

In Vieques
"The Ocean Is Closed on Mondays"

Frank the Bartender is full of information:
"So this guy, a guest, here at the hotel,
says to me, there aren't any face cloths."

So I said to him, "Sit down."

He sat down. Then I said to him, "If
you were in Paradise
would you expect to find a face
cloth?"

If you were in Paradise
would you expect to find the U.S. Navy
and the Marines bombing the hell
out of the land/mining the waters
and throwing indigenous birds, indigenous
trees, into extinction?

Where sugarcane and pineapples
and locust trees and mango and
where soursop/acacia palm
and lusciously
gardenias/amaropa/bougainvillea
grew so beautiful
in Paradise would
you expect to find the river gulleys
dried down to the dustbone of the earth/
and all the grass turned into tinderstuff?

At the hotel
Frank the Bartender says: "Jamaica?
                    No. I never had the
                        time!"

Helen and her husband Tom tell me:
"Isn't it interesting how
the Haitians are
compared to the other islander peoples

so incredibly artistic!
But do you know the story how that happened?
It was a Swede. A man named
—what was his name? *Olafson*
I'm sure: yes: Olafson.
He came, this Swede, to Haiti
and he saw the possibilities
for artistic expression among the natives
there. And he encouraged, he taught them
to do it.
That's the story!"

In Vieques there are these words painted white
on the night road

Vieques Si
Navy NO

Navy *Fuera*
(*Navy Out*)

y

Rádame Fidel Castro

At the Hotel
Frank the Bartender says:
        "So I'm with this girl down on the beach
        one night
        and I'm giving it to her
        I'm going for broke
        I'm working myself out
        pumping away
        up and down
        up and down
        and I say to her
        Is it in
        And she says
        NO
        Put it in! I yell
        So I'm going on like crazy
        Is it in? I ask her again
        Yeah, she says
        Oh, for crissakes, I tell her:
        In that case, put it back
        put it back in the sand."
I am lying on the sand

trying to relax under the spectacular sky
the Hollywood clouds looking quite superlative
in blue
y
los hombres me llaman asi:
Hey, honey
Hey, darling
ssswsssssw sssswsssw!
(Entonces)
Hey, Black Gurrl!

Last night a horse followed me home
I kept feeling there was something behind me
And there was:
A horse

His ribs glittering silver
under the tight soft colored skin of
his body, and
there wasn't any drinkable water
in sight or sound
and I noticed the hills around us dry
to the point where even Ingmar Bergman
couldn't eke out sensuality
from that ground
from the figure of that animal
standing hungry on that ground
no sensuality

and you may get the idea that the United States'
military establishment is Humphrey Bogart
cracking up all over the screen or Henry
Fonda sorry or Burt Lancaster screwing
whatshername
in the klieglit surf

but last night
this horse followed me home
in Vieques
in Paradise

and he was starved out

and as a matter of fact
this movie: the horse and the children and the
        flowers and
the fish and the coconuts and
the sea itself in Vieques

Jesus Christ!
Put it back!
Put it back!
In the sand!

The point of this movie
is
a pretty rough fuck.

Poem about a Night Out: Michael: Good-Bye for Awhile

(for Michael Harper)

There had been death There had been fire
and you would recommend Irish
whiskey saying "It's better than bourbon
smoother than scotch" and if I
replied, saying "Michael
the smoke tree sports the most infinitesimal
and linear blossomings
plus
perfectly elliptical leaves" you
might very well remark
"Uh-huh," and then inquire (the way
you did when you were pulling out the Volvo
and I ran over to the car alarmed at that)
"D'you need anything?" (gesturing to the stuff
in the backseat) "Rilke's
Duino Elegies, or anything?" the same
way you said (down to the local
disco after this guy about gave
it away to the beat that was not
that big) "Tell me
when you want me to kill him. And
I will."
There had been death There had been fire
And the last night began behind the Fleetwood
Cadillac which the disco lady owner mo-
mentarily held beside the curbstone
boxes up on Broadway and you (laughing)

dropped my letters into *Local*
while Barbara and Sonia and Robert
yelled, "Michael!"
then the saturnine the extremely pregnant
waitress told our table "If
you want anything, just wave"
while Peter rapped to me about Barbara
while Robert rapped to Barbara
about himself
while you never sat down
     you never sat down

the red rim of your ears
red throughout the whole earlier
dinnertime
red from the grieving/there had been
death there had been
fire
around the edges of your head
and here we were at five a.m. alive
alive
a silver lunacy flying small above a few
dark conifers but inside
the crowd of us was singing to the highway
well
you loved me
then you snubbed
me
now what can I do
I'm still in love with you
seeing the Japanese smoke among the mountains
then rolling into it
a u-turn on the highway
and the smoke among the mountains
and
didn't we sing
didn't we sing

Earth Angel
Earth Angel
Will you be mi-ine

and

didn't you never
never
sit down!

Poem for Inaugural Rose

Wanting to stomp down Eighth Avenue snow
or no snow where you might be so we
can takeover the evening by taxi
by kerosene lamp by literal cups of tea

that you love me

wanting to say, "Jesus, I'm glad. And I am not
calm: Not calm!" But I
am shy. And shy is short
on reach and wide on bowing
out. It's in:
against the flint and deep
irradiation of this torso listing
to the phosphorescence of French windows in
the bells/your hair/the forehead
of the morning of your face a clear
a calm decision of the light
to gather there

And you an obstinate an elegant
nail-bitten hand on quandaries of self-correction/
self-perfection as political as building your own
bed to tell the truth in
And your waist as narrow as the questions
you insist upon palpate/
expose immense not knowing any of the words
to say *okay* or *wrong*

And my wanting to say
wanting to show and tell *bells/*
okay because I'm shy
but I
will not lie

to you

Poem Nr. 2 for Inaugural Rose

Calling you from my kitchen to the one where
    you cook
for strangers and it hits me how we fall
into usefulness/change into steak or sausage or
(more frequently) fried chicken

like glut to the gluttonous/choosing a leg a poem
a voice and even a smile a breast/dark or light
    moments
of the mind: how
they throw out the rest or adjudicate the best of our
feelings/inedible because somersault singing
    in silence
will not flake to the fork at 425 or any kind of cue
will not do
and joy is not nice on ice: joy is not nice
But thinking about you over there at the stove
while I sit near the sink and we are not turkey/
I am not ham or bananas/nothing about you
reminds me of money or grist for the fist
and so on and so on but outside you know there is

rain to no purpose in the cockroach concrete of this
common predicament
and I find myself transfixed by the downpour un-
necessarily beating my blood up to the (something
    inside me
wants to say the *visual instinct of your face* or
sometimes I need to write Drums to Overcome
    the Terrors
of Iran but really
it's about the) grace the chimerical
rising of your own and secret eyes to surprise
and to surprise
and to surprise

me

This Wheel's on Fire:
The Poetry of June Jordan

BY SARA MILES

To READ THROUGH THE POETRY of June Jordan at this time is to explore the context, social and cultural and political, of the last two decades, and of the next. Her understandings, and contributions, are manifest; more difficult to name is her own stature in her land. Clearly, she is a major American writer. One of perhaps half a dozen American poets who can command audiences of over a thousand when she reads, she is the only one I know who can, time and time over, bring those audiences to their feet, cheering. Her literal activism has made her voice familiar in print, on television, in the streets, in passionate, tireless struggle. Few writers—black or white, female or male—have not been influenced by her syntax, her delivery, her concerns. A generation of young poets is coming to voice now, nurtured by her vision.

Still, Jordan's work remains outside the "mainstream" of American literature, and even disappears within the context of feminist and, to a lesser extent, black criticism. There have been no interviews with the poet in feminist magazines, though she has served as advisor and promoter for several; there has been no serious critical attention paid to her rather staggering output; there has been a comparative silence from the feminist network about her achievements. Her earlier books are either out of print or difficult to obtain; her selected poems, *Things That I Do in the Dark* (1977), representing over twenty years of work, has been barely reviewed.

This mixture of fame and invisibility is, perhaps, to some degree, the lot of any writer, and certainly of most black writers who practice their art in a white culture. But the refusal to take June Jordan's work seriously, to give it the weight it deserves, or to recognize the public confirmation of her poetry, goes beyond the bedrock racism of feminist and establishment critics alike. At a time when "backlash" against all progressive movements is swelling and progressive movements have hardened into sectarian splinter groups—at a time when the arts may be seen as decorative and many artists not seen at all, June Jordan's work must be, at least, an annoyance: and an annoyance to, among others, those sisters and brothers and comrades who cannot quite neatly contain her. Beneath Jordan's skill as an innovator, an inventor of forms, a poetic stylist of true elegance, is a vision—one clearly heard, and responded to, by her audiences—that threatens, that challenges, that must be blocked.

It is a moral vision, at base, profoundly anarchistic: one that does not sentimentalize, but roots itself in the heart. Intelligent and clear-eyed, it recognizes the interconnectedness of all life and the illegitimacy of all authority that is based on power rather than love; it is a vision revolutionary, and religious, to the core.

Put simply, the woman will not shut up. Some feminists who applauded "Poem about My Rights" for its resistance to misogynist violence and domination had trouble when the poem extended to include African self-determination; some leftists who responded to her denunciation of the United States Navy in "Poem about Vieques" were upset by the poet's apparent lack of solidarity with Puerto Rican men. June Jordan is perhaps the most deeply political poet we have, yet her poetry has never become predictably party line. She agitates and sings "from my personal and idiosyncratic and indisputably single and singular heart," which is, in fact, the heart of the people.

But it is unfair to catalog June Jordan's work by political stance, by content alone: more than any other poet, she is responsible for a dazzling marriage of form and message. She draws on American voice to create a style as unique as Whitman's, and as large. She has invented, recently, a long line that is seamless and supple and unmistakably current-America; she masters, as well, the sonnet, the throwaway couplet, the brief meditation, the lyric. Listen to the rhythm and the rhyme, the cadence of these lines from "Poem for Inaugural Rose":

> the bells / your hair / the forehead
> of the morning of your face a clear
> a calm decision of the light
> to gather there

This is music: exceptional in its beauty even for a love lyric, and exceptional as prelude to a second, still beautiful, still lyrical love poem that can contain the lines:

> we are not turkey /
> I am not ham or bananas

In much of June Jordan's work is a kind of incandescence, a charging of language so that the literal, daily, watched world is lit, from within, by history. In "Taking Care" we follow the poet as she pans across Baltimore, taking in the corner bar and the grocery store and the arguments, presented in dense detail, of assorted citizens, through what must be the longest one-breath rollercoaster of a sentence in contemporary poetry:

> in Baltimore the point about the stone steps
> the white stone stairs that women wash
> as frequently as underwear
> the point is what else
> should you try
> to take care of

And in "Poem about a Night Out: Michael: Goodbye for a While" the poet makes a gift of memory, transforming these details:

> and the last night began behind the Fleetwood
> Cadillac which the disco lady owner momentarily held beside the curbstone
> boxes up on Broadway.

She transforms them by tenderness:

> the red rim of your ears
> red throughout the whole earlier
> dinnertime

and by weaving such details, such friendship, into a pattern of context whose main thread: "There had been death There had been fire" repeats like a chant, along with the affirmation: "and here we were at five a.m. alive."

"Poem about Vieques" is a shocking masterpiece precisely because it hits on so many levels, incorporating all of these elements of June Jordan's craft: it is incontestably, and personally, political; it is lyrical, and idiomatic; it documents everyday speech and then runs a line on, stretching breath into music. "Vieques" is a poem about colonialism: the same man who says, "Jamaica? I never had the time." is the man whose vicious story about "this girl on the beach" Jordan sets down, hilariously, chillingly. As she segues into "I am lying on the sand," the impact of domination—of a woman, of an island—becomes real. The complex grids of power web up, in this poem, into a terrifying picture: the domination of the U.S.A. Navy over the island, of the American tourists over the hotel employees, of the hotel employees over the "natives," and of the "natives" over one woman, alone, "trying to relax." All of this is underscored by the destruction of natural life in Vieques, the real world raped by power, and ironically amplified by the poet's interweaving of American myths.

It is shocking that this poem should be so beautiful, that lines like:

> . . . sugarcane and pineapples
> and locust trees and mango and
> where soursop / acacia palm
> and lusciously
> gardenias / amaropa / bougainvillea
> grew so beautiful
> in Paradise . . .

should flow through a poem of such white heat, and be juxtaposed with colloquial, conversational speech. It is more shocking that the poem should be funny: that the anecdotes, the stories, the bragging and chatter should make us laugh instead of scolding us into a "correct" position of disapproval. Jordan, like Nicanor Parra, is a poet capable of being furious and funny at the same time, one whose outrageousness, whose wildness, does not diminish her accuracy or her serious rage.

Those who have seen June Jordan performing "Poem about Vieques" may have thought its epic, narrative style unprecedented, and much of the poem is new. But in 1970, with "Roman Poem Number Five," Jordan opened up this territory.

"Roman Poem Number Five" and the work that followed (including "The Talking Back of Miss Valentine Jones," "Free Flight," and others) is distinctive as poetry of many voices: voices that multiply within a single poem, not in linear sequence but almost with simultaneity. Jordan's long poems are frequently verbal collages: newspaper clippings, overheard conversations, popular songs flow through a ground that is lyrical and/or expository, using repetition, assonance, rhyme to create a whole. Her timing is perfect: the syncopation within one line will be scored, at the line break, by the entrance of a new voice.

With a vision that charges with meaning against loss, she ends the poem by reaching out:

> as we approach each other
> someone else is making a movie
> there are horses
> one or two beautiful men
> and birds flying
> away.

The moral force of June Jordan's poetry stems as much from "Roman Poem Number Five" (and from

poems like "On a New Year's Eve" (1971) where she writes "the temporary is the sacred") as from her better-known political work ("I Must Become a Menace to My Enemies," "Poem about My Rights," and "Poem against the State"). Her particularly female, particularly black, particularly American, eye sees small and large, embraces contradictions, erases boundaries.

Elsewhere, June Jordan talks about her own life and work, explaining her rejection of "either/or" formulations. To want *everything*: to stubbornly affirm the interdependence of all life, and of history; to refuse diminution and trivialization and "proper" concerns is heroic. I am moved by June Jordan's courage in undertaking to make all the connections, and awed by her skill, and grateful to be pushed so: proud, in short, to have this poet, complicated, brilliant, *alive*, alive with us.

---

* The poems referred to can be found in this anthology, in *Things That I Do in the Dark*, Random House (1977), and in *Passion*, Beacon Press (Boston, 1980).

SARA MILES was editor of the anthology *Ordinary Women* (Ordinary Women Books) while editor of that press. She has been editor and publisher of the New York City Poetry Calendar since 1976 and, before that, she was poetry editor of *Liberation* magazine in 1975. Her poems, essays, reviews, and criticism have appeared in anthologies and numerous magazines. She recently completed her poetry manuscript, "Native Dancer."

June Jordan Interview

BY KARLA M. HAMMOND

Question: June, can you envision what it might be like to be a woman in a non-patriarchal society?

JJ: This kind of language is jargon. I'm a poet and I don't talk about "patriarchal." What kind of word is that except as a joke? "Matriarchal!" Doesn't improve it. They're both ugly sounding. I can't envision a non-patriarchal society because this is all I know.

What I can envision is the possibility that enough people will come to understand that, if I have power equal to your power, you don't have less power. Because I am as happy as you have been able to be, that doesn't mean that your happiness must diminish. It doesn't have to be either/or. In 1964, when Bucky Fuller and I met for the first time, he said that the problem was that the fundamental habit of Western thought was the "either/or" formulation. It's so unimaginatively malevolent and antithetical to the nature of the universe in which we all exist. You can have a fantastic house and all the rest of it and I can, too, and it's not going to hurt you (laughs). It's going to hurt you less that I'm not hurting anymore. That's why, when the Women's Movement came to public attention, many of the spokeswomen tried to explain that the liberation of women would really liberate men. The more we had, the more they'd have. This way of thinking "both/ and," the opposite of "either/or," is really alien to Western thought, which is based on the Aristotelian concept that you cannot have "A" and "Not A" simultaneously. However, we know—even in physics—that's a fallacy, because of the Principle of Indeterminacy. You can never know where "A" is anyway (laughs).

Question: How do you respond to Audre Lorde's statement that "for women . . . poetry is not a luxury. It is a vital necessity of our existence. It forms the quality of light within which we predicate our hopes and dreams toward survival and change, first made into language, then into idea, then into more tangible action"?

JJ: I'm not sure that I know what Audre is saying. Certainly she's speaking as a poet. I know that most women are *not* poets. If she's talking about the necessity to create yourself, from your basis of self-love and self-respect in an environment hostile to your self-respect and self-love, then what she's saying is to be said about all Black people. For many people, and for many women, especially Black women, in this country, poetry is a luxury. For Audre, it is not a luxury because Audre is a poet. For me, it is not a luxury because that's my life. But I am not all women, nor am I all Black women. I have friends who don't even read poetry. However, poetry is where all of my action, thinking, feeling begins and, finally, returns. Poets name experience, and then maybe two thousand people know. But there's an outward movement of an idea that has a name, and some terrifically elaborated version of an event may come into the life of a lady sitting two doors down on a stoop (who will never read poetry) because the social worker dealing with her family has read that name. Then the social worker looks at this woman sitting on the stoop in a different way.

Question: Then there is a social responsibility in writing poetry or prose to effect changes in society?

90

JJ: Clearly, yes. . . .

At the end of the sixties everyone was questioning the Vietnam issue, doing research. In Noam Chomsky's *The New Mandarins*, he speaks about how crazy it was to sit around and say, "Well, I don't think we should have so many bombers doing this sort of thing. That's all right but not this." He felt we should just say, "This is *wrong*." He was making a moral judgment. I've done more than my share of research on the drop-out and unemployment rates. I am not interested in that anymore. I say, "You don't have children coming into the world in order for them to die by the time they're five and six years of age. This is *wrong*." I want to move on it. This attitude derives from a religious apprehension of experience. People need a sense of things that lets them say, "This is *not right*" and from that level of response make whatever move is necessary.

Question: Racial and sexual identity have traditionally been perceived to be threatening in a way that nationalistic identity is not. Why do you think that this is so?

JJ: You can't do anything about your race or your sexual identity. That's given to you. So if people will organize on the basis of what is unalterable about them, it will be serious. But nationalism, regardless of how serious it is, is not given in the same way: that's alterable. It's extremely intense but the basis of it is a phantomic collectivity. Each of us is only each of us, and each of us is either male or female, Black or White or Yellow, an irreducible factor. That lends an intensity and a passion to our concern about what happens to us, because of those things, to which any nationalistic commitment cannot compare.

Question: Black women writers have, until recently, been ignored in America and yet they've figured as a strong, central force in the family unit. What are the primary reasons the Black woman has had more difficulty getting recognition than the Black man—in the literary field, for example?

JJ: Sexism: a traditional disregard, which is not as benign as that may sound, of the potentiality of any woman who does not serve a stereotypic female function.

Question: In a recent correspondence with Ethelbert Miller, he spoke of looking at your work, Alice Walker's, Gayl Jones', Audre Lorde's, Thulani Davis' and Ntosake Shange's—looking at the concept of violence and determining whether women have been colonized by men.

JJ: I'll give you an anecdote that might be germane. I sent Ethelbert a copy of the "Poem about My Rights," and he said, "you should take your mother out of that." And I said, "Why?" And he said, "Because until you get to your mother, everything that you're talking about who has done something to you—whether it's South Africa or the guys in France—is male. It's a man in some form violating you." And I said, "Listen, I don't give a damn who it is that violates me. Violation is violation. When my mother asked me to have braces on my teeth, plastic surgery on my nose and straighten my hair, she violated me and that was the first woman I ever knew. She stays in that poem." I really have a horror of generic anything. I'm not saying that I am against the colonization of my life by men. I'm against colonization (laughs) period. I don't give a damn who does it. It's a mistake to assume that anyone—be it women, Black people or any one of us—generically speaking, has a corner on virtue. It's dangerous to think otherwise because you're deceiving yourself about your own capacities to be harmful.

Question: Would you agree with Adrienne Rich that "feminism is inextricable from socialism"? Do women have a deeper concern for, a commitment to, the environment than men do? Is the issue one of humanism versus power and money?

JJ: I hope that political states, sovereignties, and the movements that are socialistic will, in fact, attach themselves fervently to the values of Feminism. I also hope that all Feminist movements will fervently attach themselves to the values of socialism. It's difficult to understand how you can talk about each according to her need and then systematically create an under class—be it children, Black people or women. Then, on the other hand, how can you say "I don't have the time to be concerned about Southern Africa or Brooklyn or the men on the corner?"

Question: Is it important for a woman writing to-day to dissociate herself from all of the conflict of her own history or from the conflict of the Women's Movement to gain a perspective on her own writing?

JJ: No, that doesn't follow at all in a logical way. I'm not talking about being disengaged. My whole life is a political engagement. I'm talking about recognizing that, regardless of the passion, the depth or the extent of your engagement, it is only you, one person. You can only speak honestly from that reality. I'm absolutely committed to liberation struggles all over the world, but that doesn't mean that I can speak for the Vietnamese. I can speak from my understanding of their liberation struggle and its relation to my liberation struggle. I can speak *from* that, but I cannot speak *for* them. And I can only say *we* after I have made the intellectual humility, the limit of my one self, clear.

Question: In your *Chrysalis* article you speak of a "difficult, perpetual birth" in terms of one's life and one's writing. Are there any underlying principles for this?

JJ: Unless you're a fool, or arrogant, or both, you have to be born again and again and again. You're always re-evaluating what you thought you knew or what you thought was true about yourself and about other people in the world. When that takes place, very often the cumulative effect is to change you. I'm centered, but I'm not finished. If you're alive and you're not changing, you're blocked. Change is threatening, uncomfortable. The process of birth is difficult to make as a Black woman or as a woman because this birth is self-consciously undertaken and fostered. What you may want to create with yourself, or of your life, society in general may despise or condemn, as is the case in Richard Wright's *Native Son*. If he created himself in a way that was antithetical to his enemies who had all the power, then his enemies would kill him. But if he didn't create himself antithetical to the idea of himself that his enemies had put together, then he would have killed himself. In women's lives today you see that same absurdist predicament. It can only be met

moment by moment and frequently with fear and sorrow.

Question: In discussing your poetry that looks to the past (written for/to/about family members), is this an attempt at making peace with one's past (reconciliation)? Or is it an attempt to recapture something lost or elusive? (i.e., "One Minus One Minus One")

JJ: Again I don't know that it's "either/or." It could be all of those things. That poem is certainly not about making peace with the past. It's a way of attempting to deal with how you got to be here, whoever you are. Some of the ways of getting here may be very frightening. Because my mother loved me and was a good mother, to the extent that she was, she sacrificed her life. I have to deal with that; otherwise, I'm blocking a very important issue. I wrote that poem after reading Adrienne's *Of Woman Born*. I was terrified by that book, frightened by realizing that, had my mother killed me, she might have had a much more fulfilled life. But every one of us is at least also the other two people who brought us here. So it's necessary to keep going back to those two people and their relationship to each other and to you in order to really understand what you're carrying around that you call yourself.

Question: You've written familial poems and spoken of growing up in New York. What attitude or conviction of your parents' has stayed with you longest?

JJ: My father was a very proud man and a fighter. The men who knew him called him the "Little Bull" as a matter of fact. He was relatively short but very powerful. He had a flagrant and consistent contempt for the way in which other people labeled him, whether it was to call him a Negro, a Black or a West Indian. He would always say, "This is a man by the name of Granville Ivanhoe Jordan" because that was his name, not a label. That had a great impact on me. His general West Indian pride relates to having an intact ego, one not particularly vulnerable to outside manipulation. My mother was a masochist most of her life. That had enormous influence on me because it hurt and angered me to see her like that. At the same time, she was deeply religious and faithful and certainly imparted a religious sense of experience, service, and purpose. My parents had the conviction that life is a battleground. There were things that you did to win: You studied, you became very well-educated, you were quite consciously competitive. You were always trying to better yourself in ways that you could articulate. Their influence on me was particularly great while I was young. It's not as though I had a tremendous choice about whether or not to accept their value system at that time.

Question: Can you speak of some of the "eclectic compulsions" (*Chrysalis*) that you struggled against?

JJ: It was difficult for this Black poet to master a number of craft elements because the content of the poems was so alien to my experience. So I was very excited when I was finally able to do it. I wanted to say "Listen, I can alliterate for hours (laughs). I can do an iambic pentameter number that will never stop." It was a power technical display tendency that I saw in myself. It's partly showing off . . . partly to say "Yes, I am a Black poet; and yes, God damn it, I can do anything you guys can do and I can do something you can't do (laughs) because I'm Black." But, on the other hand, what I was trying to say was "Don't say she's a good poet because she's Black and she's not doing so badly." Say, "She can do anything we can do and she can do something we can't do." This was my goal, and it's related to what my father and mother always used to say to me: "You're Black and so that means you can't be a good student. You've got to be twice as good a student as anyone else. You have to be the best athlete, the most popular, the best looking, etc. You know why?—in order to qualify as a B grade candidate of any other description racially." Do you know what I'm saying? You have to do all of this in order to say "I'd really like to go to City College. Is it all right?" (laughs) So that was the attitude I transferred to poetry. I didn't want anyone patronizing me, saying "She's really doing pretty well, but she's a Black poet." I'd say, "Let's make the comparison on a strictly technical level and I'll hold my own." That was my goal. I was

excited about words *per se* (which have always excited me, deliriously at times), but also I was excited about all those things that I now knew how to do. I thought "God!" You can get into what I call pyro-technical ecstasy which is quite irrelevant to statement (laughs).

Also underlying everything about my art—poetry—is a tremendous concern for beauty. What craft knowledge makes possible is the creation of beautiful things. Shirley Clark and I worked together on the film "A Cool World" (about Harlem before the sixties), and she said that what I'm talking about is really a problem. If you're talking about something horrifying or agonizing, then, because of your craft, you're going to talk about what is really beautiful. She had pictures of these young Black kids walking down garbage-lined streets—garbage that should be picked up and housing that is garbage standing up. But in shooting the film she waits until it's dark, and raining. So the street is slick and luscious, looking almost like a fruit that they're walking upon. And you think "God, is that beautiful." But that's not the purpose of that film. The purpose of that film is to say, "These children are dying and we are the ones murdering them."

Or suppose it's an irreversible rhythm in a poem. I'm saying, "The boy who should be alive is dead now." I want you to understand that, and to say it in a way that will not be beautiful but that will have all the effectiveness that my craft can let me accomplish. That's what I meant by "eclectic compulsions," all the ways in which you learn to make your use of language beautiful regardless of the subject matter, regardless of the ideational intent of the work. If you don't resist it, sometimes you can risk making pretty what is truly despicable.

Question: You've spoken of Shelley and Coleridge as "unalterable" influences. For the benefit of anyone who hasn't yet read "Thinking about My Poetry" (*Chrysalis*), could you speak of some of the influences that have changed?

JJ: I used to be interested in Shakespeare's poetry and plays. Now that I've learned from him what I needed to learn, I'm not really that interested in doing many of those things that followed from such a study. T. S. Eliot also had an enormous influence on me at one point. I was really self-consciously imitating him. Then I stopped and read him for content and realized I didn't give a damn. "The women come and go talking of Michelangelo." It was very effective to express this grief of non-event. But I knew that, for myself, if I'm going to say "da dum da dum da dum da dum da dum," I'm going to use that technique to say, "Listen, every single second that has to do with a human being is important." So even apart from his anti-Semitism, the man was not consecrated to the important. He didn't believe in the holiness of life, not even in his own life, which he took care of with such luxury. Eliot was dangerous because his langorous meter, his work, was very seductive, especially for me at sixteen.

Then LeRoi Jones (*Dead Lecturer: Poems*) had a great impact on me. Those are still wonderful poems for me—this extremely lucid articulation of ambivalence. I was infatuated with many different concepts of ambivalence, but I'm no longer so fascinated by ambivalence. When I read Langston Hughes and some of what Baraka (LeRoi Jones) began to do later on that was regarded as distinctively Black, it influenced me in a funny way. I decided that it was perhaps an unduly limited and patronizing view of the possibilities of a Black aesthetic. I wasn't going to have anyone Black or White tell me what it would mean for me to be a distinctively Black poet. I would decide that for myself, just trusting the fact that I am Black, that I grew up in Bedford-Stuyvesant, and that whatever I arrive at will be authentic. It

wouldn't be feigned or strictly intellectual. It would come from everything that I am, and it will be more than a kind of unilateral, spoken use of language. It will be more than a castigation of enemies. It will be more than that because we (Black people) are more than all of that.

Another influence of whom I can speak is Margaret Walker. That influence hasn't changed. Her poem "For My People" is one of a kind: I was tremendously excited when I first saw it many years ago. The only other person who has written a poem of that magnitude might be Rimbaud—in some of his so-called prose poetry. They both give poetry the kind of condensed power that only it yields. At the same time, the essential factors of her poem, "For My People," and some of Rimbaud's prose poetry are rhetorical. Mallarme, Rimbaud, and Jacques Prevert used to have a great influence on me, just for the sound in French. Also Gertrude Stein. At one time they were enormously in the forefront of my attention for technical reasons and the pleasure that they gave me. Now I'm consciously preoccupied in different ways.

KARLA HAMMOND has interviewed over thirty-five other women poets, doing all research, typing, transcription, and editing herself. Interview editor for *The Bennington Review*, she also freelances interviews and writes reviews, criticism, and fiction. Her poems have been published in over 100 literary magazines here and abroad.

June Jordan: Biographical Notes

All of this started with my uncle. He was a probation officer, living with my aunt and her daughter on the third (top) floor of our Brooklyn brownstone. Even when he washed and polished his car on weekends, my uncle sported a pistol, most of the time,

and told amazing, terrific stories. I adored him, and he liked me well enough. After his tour in World War II, as a second lieutenant stationed mainly in Georgia, he brought back for me, as a very special present, a rather lusty full-grown raccoon.

During childhood I was relatively small, short: a target for bully abuse. My father was the first regular bully in my life; there were many days when my uncle pounded down the two flights of stairs to grab the chair, the knife, or whatever, from my father's hands.

But outside intervention has its limits. My uncle decided to teach me how to fight for myself. He showed me numerous ways to disarm/disable an assailant. But what he told me is what I best remember: "It's a bully. Probably you can't win. That's why he's picking the fight. But if you go in there, saying to yourself, 'I may not win this one but it's going to cost you. Because I'll be going for your life'—if you go in there like that, they'll leave you alone. And remember: it's a bully. It's not about fair. From the start, it's not about fair."

I learned, in short, that fighting is a whole lot less disagreeable than turning tail or knuckling under. I lost a lot of fights as a kid, in Bedford Stuyvesant. But nobody ever fought me twice. They said I was "crazy."

While my uncle was teaching me pugilistics, my parents were teaching me the Bible. My mother carried me—I must have been two or three years old—to the Universal Truth Center on 125th St. every Sunday before we moved from Manhattan. That early on, the Scriptural concept: "In the beginning was the Word and the Word was with God and the Word was God"—the idea that the word could represent and then deliver into reality what the word symbolized—this possibility of language, or writing, seemed to me magical and basic and irresistible.

I loved words and I hated to fight. But if, as a Black girl-child in America, I could not evade the necessity to fight, maybe I could choose my weaponry at least.

It was the week after the Harlem Riot of 1964, a week of lurching around downtown streets like a war-zone refugee, that I realized I now was filled with hatred for everything and everyone White. Almost simultaneously it came to me that this condition, if it lasted, would mean I had lost the point: not to resemble my enemies; not to dwarf my world; not to lose my willingness and ability to love.

So, back in 1964, I resolved not to run on hatred but, instead, to use what I loved, words, for the sake of the people I loved. This propelled me into a reaching far and away to R. Buckminster Fuller, to whom I proposed a collaborative architectural redesign of Harlem, as my initial, deliberated movement away from the hateful, the divisive. Our first meeting lasted several hours, just the two of us, alone. We would think and work together to design a three-dimensional, exemplary life situation for Harlem residents. This was a way of looking at things that escaped the sundering paralysis of conflict by concentrating on the purpose of the fight: What kind of schools, streets, parks; what kind of privacy, beauty, music; what kind of options would make love a reasonable, easy response?

My life seems to be an increasing revelation of the intimate face of universal struggle. You begin with your family and the kids on the block, and next you open your eyes to what you call your people and that leads you into land reform, into Black English, into Angola, leads you back to your own bed where you lie by yourself, wondering if you deserve to be peaceful or trusted or desired or left to the freedom of your own unfaltering heart. And the scale shrinks to the size of a skull: your own interior cage.

And then, if you're lucky, and I have been lucky, everything comes back to you. And then you know why one of the freedom fighters in the sixties, a young Black woman interviewed shortly after she was beaten up for riding near the front of an interstate bus—you know why she said, "We are all so very happy."

It's because it's on. All of us and me by myself: we're on.

JUNE JORDAN

* This autobiographical material also appears as the foreword to Jordan's book *Civil Wars: Selected Essays 1960–1980* (Beacon Press, 1981).

*

June Jordan, born in Harlem July 9, 1936, was educated at Barnard College and the University of Chicago. Her poems, articles, essays, and reviews have frequently appeared in *Black World*, *Ms.*, *The New York Times*, *The New Republic*, *The Nation*, *Essence*, *Partisan Review*. Her son, Christopher David, is a student at Harvard. Currently, she is Associate Professor of English at the State University of New York at Stony Brook. She has won many prizes, the most recent being a 1981–82 grant from the National Endowment for the Arts.

In addition to her four new books in one year—November 1980–1981, she is the author of a full-length drama, *The Issue*, centered on police violence in the black community. Her recent books are *Civil Wars: Selected Essays 1960–1980* (Beacon Press, 1981); *Kimako's Story*, a children's book (Houghton Mifflin & Company, 1981); *Passion: New Poems, 1977–1980* (Beacon Press, 1980); *Things That I Do in the Dark: Selected Poems, 1958–1977*, a revised edition (Beacon Press, 1981).

Kristina McGrath

NEW YORK, NEW YORK

Sequence from Blue to Blue

The Hour in April

You are sitting
in a room
preparing for something
in the usual blue
company of nothing
you are having the idea

of a woman moving
transparent, slice of air
you will give it back
in the blind exercise
of your breathing

your voice is narrow
you lead her in
she takes on the appearance
of trees in the empty season

but still you insist
there are bones
at the shoulder

seen through a half-remembered
windowglass crippled with water
her thinness or yours
splinters the air
you are a woman too
you understand this

commotion under your palms
an hour is the length of her body
and you know what happens next

you will lose her and then you do
the handprint, her signature

floats on the wall
you count the blue grains
of snow from her fingertips
but still you insist

the bone, the evidence
glistens
at the bottom of the river.

The Afternoon in May

Suddenly
she is sitting
by the river
crosslegged
in the emptiness
prepared for her
on the grass
or in your life
this is the first time.

You recognize her at once
you are there in the shade
of her voice.

I know what I want, she says
her handprint on the water is white
she makes the river white
with the palm of her hand
and you know what happens next.

You've seen this before   this

97

was the unlived afternoon
transparent in light

That lasted
an hour or a long time
and then you let it go.

White cargo
from the drowning branches
tangles in the river
odor of light
white blossom.

I know what I want, she says
I know what there is
whatever is left.

The slender white
rag inside the pear
for example
the tree that's a bone
by tomorrow at the bottom
of this river not that it matters
eventually, the clean discovery
of darkness and your hands
around my waist.

The Nights in June

Late at night
that sort of thing

her spine
in the palm of your hand
in the curve of your palm
where she puts it
and you cannot
give it back

the heartbeat, the invitation
wrapped in the sheets.

By July

By July
she's become a matter
of breathing
a difficulty
climbing up and down
the white dream, the blue dream
in her heart you get a footing
your hands around the waist of someone

who says
she is not
staying
her waist or yours
is the slender white
rag inside the pear
and you know what happens next
she will lose you.

August

I know what there is, she says
I know what I want

when she touches
you in the darkness
it is her way
of touching
the darkness   her handprint
on the river is blue

she makes the river blue
with the palm of her hand.

Sharon Olds

NEW YORK, NEW YORK

Thomas Victor

Homage

Zoya Kosmodemyanskaya,
18-year-old Russian partisan
executed by the Nazis,
November, 1941

I know. You don't want to hear about it,
and I don't want to think about it
but there it is: her body lies frozen in the snow
in a field near Moscow, the rope still around her
    neck,
stiff in the sub-zero air.
They have pulled up the rough white cloth of her
    shirt
to show where they dug out one of her breasts.
There is snow in the coarse excavation,
snowflakes on her eyelashes
and defiant grieving lips, and on the long
curve of her broken neck.
Her chopped hair is dark against the crust,
and moves in the wind.
    I want to say:
let no one turn away.
Her tilted darkened face is beautiful,
her throat, her one nipple. I want us to stop

and think about her for a moment,
think of nothing but her.

The Mole

My girl found it on the way to the garden,
its hands raised in surprise, its head
turned away. With the trowel, I touched it
gently and it was awful soft,
black fur silky and pliant as
Grandmother's seal coat. Against that
darkness, its pointed paws stuck out
like ivory knitting needles, its face
horribly pained, little mouth
sour against the huge piece of
locust bark fallen across it.
We knelt too long on either side of the
small body, then buried it
and went along to the garden. I felt
sick, as if some smooth black
knowledge had passed between us—
as if I had admitted to her
that I know I will die or, worse yet,
that I know she will die, my dark sleek
secretive daughter.

Ellen Wittlinger

CAMBRIDGE, MASSACHUSETTS

Waiting

First you wait for yourself
at the top of the staircase, thinking,
am I all right now, is it
time? You fight the undertow of fear,
then try to find the zero in yourself
and start back up from there.
You continue down the stairs.

There's no one waiting for you
at the designated spot
so you wait. Your attention flies
like birds after the first gunshot
afraid to land anywhere and crazy
to migrate. Finally you let the mind
settle and hide in some easy detail
of a table, a lamp,
the cover of a magazine.
You can't help noticing the ring marks
on the table, deliberately yours,
unadmitted heretofore,
and the grammatical error
in the headline that first caught your eye.
Life's harmless mistakes
seem to multiply.

There comes the time when you must rise
and look out the window. The dark
holds such hope, you had such hope earlier,
when you tied the red scarf around your neck.
You imagined the night; for a moment
you expected miracles. But now you look out
at the wet, quiet street and you wait
for the headlights to stop,
to burn up your eyes.

And yet, what if he were to come now
and find you like this, on the verge
of coming open, drawing with your fingers
on the window? You must arrange yourself.
Sit casually on one hip, as though you expected
nothing, have a smile ready,
just inside your lips. Just once
practice turning your face
to the door, where he could enter, late,
and change hope into truth
with one embrace.

All you can do is wait.
In the silence of waiting you become
cold, numb. Suddenly
you hope he doesn't come.
Your hands have become so happy
with each other, resting in your lap.
Your smile relaxes and saves itself
for no one. You have such a clear
picture of your own body, posed,
waiting forever for some famous painter
to finish. It's as though you stand quietly
behind a crack in the door, watching her,
the maniacal you, demanding
she will wait forever.

In Cahoots

If only we knew each other!
If only you had a nose like Frank
O'Hara, I might feel lucky, I might
throw away an old rabbit's foot
that's kept me safe for years.

If only we were in cahoots somehow
and slowly you began to interfere
with my life, and I couldn't take a bath
without noticing what a stranger
I am. If only I were a kid
in the grocery store and you were
an older boy in the neighborhood
who remembered my name,
I would pose like a show-off
before my own mirror, alone,
happy with my big future.

Someone You Love

Sometimes the rumor of a death
just beginning in someone
reaches you in the early evening
when you're most at ease
with life and vulnerable.
You've had your coffee, you're going
for a short walk and then he tells you:
another ending has begun.
The grief of endings overtakes you.
You remember why you cried
to leave home even for a month
and will cry harder on the thirty-first
to go back. And as you unpack
you'll see his face in every folded
article which no longer fits
in your drawer: everywhere he's touched you
glows. Everyone who touches you knows:
someone you love has death in him.

For a moment you can't help feeling
your own heart could be a healer,
could stop a mere disease
with massive love.
But all your wild ideas wither
on your tongue. You watch him
face it, waste nothing,
charm the unsuspecting with his laugh.
The grief of endings overtakes you
like an echo

that will never stop coming back.
Someone you love has death in him
and there is nothing you can do but leave.

Red

My friend who haunts antique stores says
he'll look for the red dress I described,
the one in my first memories that made
my mother beautiful, her red lips slide
over each other like water and ice, shine
like unreachable fruit
in the top of the tree. I say: the feel
of wool in my hand, the way
she looked at herself in the mirror
like a judge. And I see him
daring himself to tell his own story.

Still, he will not shelter under the umbrella
with me, claims the spring rain warms
winter skin. We discuss fashion,
the muted silks of this year's sophisticates.
He knows clothes.
Since childhood I've said *red*,
and I repeat it to him now, the challenge,
Red. He leaps
from the dead pool of conversation
and agrees, *yes, red, red, red*.
His hair is wet, making him less than perfect.

Like my mother I am very ordinary, no one
would look twice. I need the dress
or the dream of the dress to make new dreams.
I would like my own child
to see me in the dress or someone just on the edge
who could fall in love with the real me.
I brush his hand accidentally.
He fills his eyes and empties them.
As he leaves I put down the umbrella, one
last show of weakness. "I'll look," he says.
"Such olive skin you have,
that red becomes you."

Akua Lezli Hope

BROOKLYN, NEW YORK

Baron James Ashanti

No One Comes Home to Lonely Women

she runs coatless
colder than winter
no metaphor for why.
burning agonies must keep her warm
behind the wild whorl she uses as eyes
it is Riviera with the Italian dude
she bragged, maddened by her dark
wine and pixie face
bagged by close ensnaring wind of her hair
scent of dusky kush cotton
Romans always was collectors
or maybe its spring wid her Black collegiate
his big thing and campus women
green eyein', dyin' for her to go back home
was it bad mens?
could be summer again
teachin art to project kids
slidin to home plate through wine bottles
salaried enough to keep tryin
dumb enough to care.
where we met
she was Black Phoebe
near peer, lark ascending
was it frustrations?
Madness did not steal her youth:
under a sullen rusty wig
a pixie glimmer haunts her face
Pat is that you head in washing machine
enclosed in remote glee of some unheard joke

God does protect fools: not one
panty nor suds fell out machines' mindless whirl
she slow straightened (the other pushed aside)
assumed a still remembered attitude of spine,
    shoulder
and eye flashed recognition and spoke
bourgie chitchat lingo

why didn't i grab you then
slap or hold you
could no one love you?

i didn't know her well enough to cry
but knew enough to wonder why
how she be like SRO men
state's waste howling
on slush streetcorners
at noon high and mid/night

she sails down Broadway
defiance in her chestchin thrust
mute compliance in bare, crossed arms

reach for just bought coffee
look for a five—can't spare a dime
i run slow-mo heavy boots
three-pair socks two sweaters
ten ton coat . . .

and like Billy Bessie Zora

she is gone.

1978

To Sister for Mother

"O!" her daughter cried,
"Hope can *think*."

Even if she settles doesn't mean she
can't select. The simple stitch well
worked holds firm each thread
needs not express but builds
a subtle art. Call it genius.
Things which last. Heard by heart.

1979

Ann Lauterbach

NEW YORK, NEW YORK

Diana Michener

The Yellow Linen Dress:
A Sequence

I

A solemn discourse is not necessary
although I am inclined
to triumph and exalted states
that remind me of mother at her best:
how everything about her was sheer.
This is my habit, to come through
vanity—through her—
and to sweep away the ribbons
she shed as she sailed into image.
She had a ring around her, but was not religious.

II

The miraculous is no more than what
comes naturally after
cold weather: this large hat
and these motherhoods
that glide to an early stop on the boulevard.
Her best was fugal: she moved
from place to place and then went back
to pick the inevitable.
I stopped bothering after a while,
leaving her to impinge on her garden.

III

He waits for her to arrive
in the family carriage.
He has heard she has beautiful hair
that she pins to her neck like a cloud.
He wears a white suit and straw hat.
He thinks the rich have bad taste

but is unsure, ambitious at heart.
The carriage arrives; she turns her head.
He thinks he will marry her, take her
on his boat, his incertitude.

IV

Rain on the lawn falls softly,
softly falling, the falling rain.
I begin to see how mannered feelings are,
dispatched to the eye of the beholder.
"I turned my head to show
how beautiful my hair is.
He stood on the porch and thought
he would marry me. We sailed away
on his boat. I sat on the deck
and watched the sun rise. It was ugly and pink."

V

A birdless sky, seadawn, one lone star,
is what she saw
as she sat on deck while he slept below.
She thought it was disgusting.
They had five daughters and now
she reads the same book over and over.
It gives her solace; she hates surprises.
Her daughter ran off and turned into ashes.
I sit on the bed. We talk of the weather.
Her hair is pinned to her neck like a cloud.

VI

I sit on the bed.
The ashes have been dumped at sea.
I have come back as part of the estate.
We do not mention the flutter
that hurries late summer into fall

or name the departed.
We will not name the departure, as
a leaf among many. She feeds the birds
at breakfast, her hair
a cloud full of mild and muttering rain.

VII

Her daughter wore a linen dress and
pearls. She sat for her portrait.
She turned her head to show
how the eye of the beholder is
forgotten. I came back
too late: she had turned into ashes.
I sat on the bed and thought:
I am going to sink her, softly, softly,
sink her. And as soon as the rain falls,
forget her. We talked of the weather.

VIII

The temptation is to shred it,
to tear it to ribbons.

Otherwise it is her father's boat
and I write to articulate
the drift of smoke between her fingers.
She was the occasion of weather:
her mother's hair full of rain.
The surface vanished, leaving a profile.
He stood on the porch behind the gate.
She followed the inhibited ferry.

IX

Everything is hers: she went through it.
She played at the gate, fearful.
She made solemn flight
in the absence of a father.
She could lie. She could write
with lips, eyes, hair,
and the way she did it
indicated how I was to follow, how
the sequel to her would be discourse
made from an inhibited, necessary image

Barbara Howes

NORTH POWNAL, VERMONT

Shunpike

(A byway; side road. *Rare.*
Webster's International
Dictionary, 1927)

Stridor! Trucks hurl themselves
At the black tarpaulin
Of highway, battering
Till it quakes, shivers, drizzles
Hot air. Noise grows upward—
From its tarmac bed—
Blasting our ears, while all that
Displaced wind treats my car
As featherduster.
Wham!
An oil-truck, non-flammable,
Shifts gears, skins the concourse
Clean, while the outer lane spews pits.

A factory in motion; on
The road, giant castanets
Beat, mile after mile,
Till the blue exit:—
Foood, fule, tel.—If we can

Sidle over white lines before the
Rear-view behemoth
Smashes, we may—empty, bloodless—
Dial to someone the high
News of our survival.

A Point of View

for Cary

Up the broad southern stair
I climbed, as always, in dream
leaned,
warmed to this
weathered tedesco
Wood on a landing, turned
right, left, to join
What led to full air. We name
People as we move along. A staunch
Room awaited, in truth, in dream,
with my love,
A ceiling high as the mind:
"I want to *know*!"

Irena Klepfisz

BROOKLYN, NEW YORK

Judy Waterman

Contexts

(for Tillie Olsen)

I

I am helping proofread the history
of a dead language. I read out loud
to an old man whose eyes have failed
him. He no longer sees the difference
between a period or a comma, a dash
or a hyphen, and needs me for I under-
stand how important these distinctions are.

The room is crammed with books, books
he had systematically tagged for future
projects—now lost. Sounds pour out
of me. I try to inject some feeling
and focus, concentrate on the meaning
of each linguistic phrase. On the edge
of my vision, he huddles over a blurred
page, moves his magnifying glass from line
to line, and we progress. Time passes.
My voice is a stranger's, sensible and
calm, and I, the cornered, attentive hostess,
listen in silence as it conjectures the his-
tory of languages long dead without a trace.
How, I wonder, did I become what I am not?

I request a break. The sounds cease.
I check the clock, calculate, write
figures in a notebook. I am numb
and stiff, walk up and down the hall,
stare into busy offices. I wait.
I wait for something forgotten, something
caught and bruised: a brown feather,
a shaft of green light, a certain word.

I bend, drink water, remember stubborn
clams clinging to the muddy bottom.

II

The building across the street
has an ordinary facade, a view of the park
and rows of symmetrical spotless windows.
Each morning, the working women come to
     perform
their duties. They are in starched white,
could pass for vigilant nurses keeping
order and quiet around those about to die.
And each morning, idle women
in pale blue housecoats, frilled and fluffed
at the edges, stare out of double windows,
waiting for something to begin.

With whom would you change places, I ask
myself, the maid or the mistress?

III

The clock sucks me back. I calculate the loss,
return to the books, his unrecognizing eyes.
He is unaware of the pantomime outside,
feels no rage that I and the world are lost
to him, only mourns the words dead on the page.
We begin again. I point to the paragraph,
synchronize the movement of eye and mouth,
abandon all pretense of feeling. Silently I float
out, out toward the horizon, out toward the open
     sea,
leaving behind the dull drone of an efficient
     machine.

                              I am
there again, standing by the railing, watching

107

the whales in their narrow aquarium, watching
their gleaming grace in the monotonous circle,
        watching
how they hunger for fleshly contact, how the young
        keeper
places his human hand in their rough pink mouths,
rubs their tongues, splashes them like babies. I
        cannot
watch them enough, but feel deeply ashamed for I
        know
the price.

With a shock I realize we are not together,
that he is lost, caught in a trap.
He sounds the words over and over, moves
the glass back and forth, insists there is
a lapse in meaning. I sit silent, tense, watch
as he painfully untangles the subtle error, watch
as he leans back exhausted saying: "I knew
        something
was wrong! I knew from the context that something
was wrong!"

IV

At the end of the day I stack the galleys,
mark an *x* where we've been forced to stop.
He is reluctant to let me go, anxious, un-
certain about the coming days, but I smile,
assure him they'll be all the same. Alone,
I rush for the bulb-lit train, for the empty
corner of the crowded car, then begin the struggle
against his sightless eyes, against the memory
of a vacant stare.

It is a story, I tell myself, at least
a story, that one Sunday when I refused
to go to work. Fifteen, bored with inventory

and week-end jobs, I stayed in bed and,
already expert, called in sick. Her rage
was almost savage, wild. She paced
through the apartment, returned to me again
and again saying *"Get up! Get up now!"*
as if I was in mortal danger. But nothing
would move me from my bed, from the sun
cutting through the iron fire escape outside,
from the half-finished book about the man
and the whale. "It's not that much money,"
I called to her.

And then her inexplicable silence. At first
she sat in the kitchen, fingering the piece
of cloth, staring absently at the teacup.
Finally she got up, began pinning the pattern.
Soon I heard the clean sound of the scissor
against the kitchen table, then silence again
as she basted. Much later that day, she worked
on the machine, and still she did not speak
to me, just let the bobbing needle make its own
uninterrupted noise. And as I went to bed
flushed with the excitement of that sea of words,
filled with my own infinite possibilities, she
continued sewing, fulfilling her obligation
for the next day's fitting.

V

The blind man balances easily in the rocking
car. He moves among us, sings, shakes a tin
cup. Most of us think it's all a con, but it
makes no difference. Pose is part of necessity.
Riding each evening through the echoing tunnels,
I've begun to believe in the existence of my own
soul, its frailty, its ability to grow narrow,
small. I've begun to understand what it means
to be born mute, to be born without hope of speech.

Kathleen Lignell

STOCKTON SPRINGS, MAINE

To Say Whose Side
You're on

Those white New England winters—
seductive and alien to me
as calendars were when as a child,
I copied those snowy scenes
with a white crayon on colored paper
near San Francisco. There was snow
and cerulean blue sky
that branched out from the maples
in the three months of official winter
pictured on the wall.
They did not look much like Mt. Diablo,
purple with lupines, or muscular foothills
yellow with wild mustard in the January rain.
You were always the same. Yankee
in a landscape I had never seen,
stone walls buried in snow
beyond what we become: a stretch
of circled holidays that assume
the shapes of seasons.

It's summer again
at the end of the world.
I wonder what to make of myself
attempting to live on the North Atlantic.
The apples are overloaded.

The women who wait for their babies
are overdue in a steamy August. The elms
still creak under all that weight.
I walk the rocky coastline
thinking of home, like the first settlers
of the eighteenth century,
who for hundreds of years, have hauled
lumber out of the forests of Maine.
A Christmas
of endless pointed fir.

White on white, out
as far as the mind can see offshore,
Willa Cather, your resident writer,
bundled in an old wool sweater
in a cabin on Grand Manan,
describes each mesa
by its Indian name, recalls
the flowering cactus of New Mexico
whose sharp prick the horny fingers
of our Spanish forebears never touched,
and Death slowly overtakes the Archbishop.
I am thinking of her, Willa,
as I watch that Canadian island appear
and disappear in its daily mirage.
I think of her pen
moving across the white paper, her long arms
reaching out for America.

Sara Miles

BROOKLYN, NEW YORK

Native Dancer

It's snowing today in the last great
capitalist city. Six times around the old
block and I'm stuck
wondering
who else is frying on this cold grey grid and God
against the same wide wall where all
of us are raising voice/shout and shudder/gets the word:
Lord
I want to go home.

Who else was watching when I saw the native
dancer: sneakers, pants
too tight/the night a sick surrender and the tender
of the trash-can fire passed wine around/ the dancer
in the dark
park
getting winter
getting drunk:
who else saw
her hands?

I want *how many people are residing here who* to go *have
no other home?* home *how many I are between the ages* want
to *of four and* go home *twelve? Who owns this? How many people*
I want to *are related* go I want to go I want to go
to each other in this place? home

Lost and found. Six times around the broken
circle and I'm wondering who
will tell me how this all will look: snow
on the water smoke on the snow: after the war

And back to the wall where no one is native the dancer

stands
hands
in her pockets/shake and shiver/deliver
me Lord
let me out
let me in I need to know
how we go home.

More

There wasn't time between the way
you placed my hands around you
in the night and then the day
you told me, go away, get out
of here there wasn't room the closer
that you came and then
retreated much too tight for me to say
that I had meant to leave, clear out,
and leaving leave a note:
If you can read this you are too close.

I sat down to write you a letter. It went:
I can't stand
how your hand is on me. And how
it isn't: Please

come home. And who
are you that then I mailed it
to myself: dear familiar, I'm turning
blue with cold in here.
Get out.

You could never be too close for comfort.
Only now when one is
both of us then three's
a crowd I'm thinking all
the masses moving history don't
use this much room. How
did it get so tight? I say, and leave
a note: if you
can read this, please
come closer.

Talking about It

"Oh muther" sings the Chinese dishwasher, 2*am*, "I'm tired
and I want to go home." last night the guy with the black
pants sang "tongues
off the leash" three of them were singing it, two men, one woman, now
I'm tired and want to go home "Chan" I say, cleaning up
scraping the grill "what are these words *Sailor Geo
graphy Vacation* are these yours" on the scrap of paper towel
by the sink, "English lesson" he says: what
are   these   words   tongues
off the leash tonight two men follow me one on each
side it's 2*am* mother I'm leaving
the restaurant they are walking very close one
on each side they are speaking words to me
what are these words
baby bitch I'm walking faster "bitch" what
is this laughing they are laughing and I stop

say stop say stop: rain. late taxis. say stop here
is the corner of the Avenue of the Americas. here
is the man beside me with his tongue out. here are no words lessons
like *Vacation* just this face up the eyes hard close up
the tongue out tongue lolling the hand moving
off the leash
I never made this
I never wanted to go
home, mother, I'm so tired, to this gate where two men
stand *2am* the words "we'll wait for you" the tongue rolling
the eyes rolling hard marbles rain like sweat like rain what
are the words on this corner beneath the tongues of these men's
faces I want off the face
of the earth moving toward me *Geography*
say stop: stop:
"bitch" here is the corner here is the lesson *Sailor*
the end of the words singing the end of the leash
pulled tight around my neck sweat
get off my neck off my back back off tongue back give me
back my own tongue and cut this off—

Honor Moore

NEW YORK, NEW YORK

Joan Potter

Poem: For the Beginning

Noon, the sky gray, the snow not falling in earnest, so
the day seems odd, too usual, almost boring, the light
    from the slight new cover on the old snow not
broken, played by the sun with color, but flat, intensely
    white. This morning a woman was saying,
        separation is good for
    love. She has been here a month, I two days, and
this new snow on old ice is slippery: I have fallen
twice. Weeks ago, I said, I want to be only happy
    with you, and you said, there are always other
feelings. What I mean is, I want to care for you, care as
        for the most delicate plant or creature, care
        as one guards a singular
    gift which is fragile, beautiful. Last night, on
the telephone, we tried to arrange your visit. You
couldn't say definitely yes, because a nearly past
    love will visit, and you must see her, so you
cannot tell me yes, definitely, this day, because
        she has not said definitely, yes, that
        day. Last night on a pay phone,
    we talked an hour, bare bulb dangling, giving
light, I tracing my returned dime with purple ball point,
moving the dime, drawing in its circle first a face,
    then hair. I say I don't trust what happens when
you are with her, scribble out eyes, mouth, move the dime, trace
        another. I'm feeling what might be my
        love for you like a change in
    temperature, wondering if I must be unsure
to feel it. This circle stays hollow. I scratch out from
its edge, flames, as if the sun were purple, eclipsed by a white
    dime moon. I wish she'd disappear, I say, and
regret it. Let's not talk about her, you say, your hair

flooding my mind like coal-colored water,
black, rushing from thick ice
on the river in town, black tongue flooding out
from white lips, endless, thawing. I want to be only
happy with you, not held back. I want to care for you as
for a delicate plant. I want you to care
for me. A woman near the fire says, I have found love
this way between women: a see-saw, one up,
the other . . . Care for you as
I want to hold you, my legs firm, your body
resisting their force, care as I want my mouth moving
against yours, as it does, as it has against no one else's
mouth, care as I want to lie beside you, our
faces close, dark, and look into you through your cordovan
eyes. *Separation is good for . . . This way . . .*
a see-saw . . . Jealousy and
possession, the woman says, are our least
legitimized feelings. *You to care for me.* This
day, light stays the same, trees don't move—silence, then an
occasional creak, the oil burner
roaring, measuring time by cold and heat—on, off, on . . .
The six-pronged shell, gift from you, balances
on its transparent stand, seems
to float, image of heat, pink center of heat
burning out, still and continuing, as if the hot
color of a daylily opening were heat rather
than color. This cold between us is distance,
circumstance. Just how, I ask her, is separation good?
Going away, she says, coming back—almost
waving her hand as she speaks.
I like coming back, leaving and coming back. Coming back.

Abundance and Scarcity

My thin mother began it at the bottle,
taunted my weight as I sucked, not Perrier
which might have kept my lengthening bones
visible, but Guernsey milk rich as Italian
cheesecake. Hence, I'm a dieter: this one, two
days in, prescribes a two day fast to shake

you down. Monday afternoon I shake
approaching the icebox: a dozen bottles
aqua minerale. My tongue's begun to
discern shades of flavor: Is Perrier's
bouquet fruitier than the Italian
Pellegrino's? or mirage, like the beef bones

I hallucinate sipping bouillon? Bones
through broth, fruit through the juice I shake
with Fiuggi till it's like Italian
soda. If at noon I call those bottles
lunch and, at six, supper, then Perrier
and Evian seem less unlike the food to

which I'm freed Wednesday: paté, two
corn dripping butter, lamb chops gnawed to the bone,
chocolate mousse . . . Guilt sweats me awake: Perrier,
thank God, and juice were all I took. The scales shake
as I mount, thighs eight pounds less like bottles
now; it's not a dream: I'll wear the Italian

silk jersey dress only an Italian
would drape me in—its folds give graciously to
humor passions for pasta *al pesto*, bottles
of good chianti. But since I miss the bones
my mother praised, want not to see a shaking
derriere mirrored in shop windows, Perrier's

the fizz through which I taste champagne, Perrier,
what fills my silver mug, my Italian
shoe; banana and yogurt the best shake;
yogurt the preferable cream; broiled the way to
render fish most luscious; plain chicken boned
and pounded the ecstasy that bottles

yearning for Escoffier that makes me shake, salivate too
much to resist bottles of champagne (Perrier et Jouet)
or meals, Italian and French, that bury bones.

Barbara Guest

SOUTHAMPTON, NEW YORK

John Ross

Quilts

"Couch of space"

Thought nest where secrets bubble
through the tucking, knowing what it's like outside,
drafts and preying beasts, midnight plunderers
testing your camp site and the aery demons, too,
waiting to plunge their icy fingers into your craw
and you crawl under, pull the quilt on top
making progress to the interior, soul's cell.

Following the channel through shallows
where footsteps tremble on quicksand squiggly
penmanship of old ladies, worms with cottony
spears, the light pillared the way trees crowd
with swallows and then a murmur in the ear
as deeper flows the water. The moon comes out
in old man dress, thoughtfully casts an oar.

You float now tideless, secure in the rhythm
of stuffing and tying, edging and interlining,
bordered and hemmed; no longer unacquainted
you inhabit the house with its smooth tasks
sorted in scrap bags like kitchen nooks
the smelly cookery of cave where apples
ripen and vats flow domestic yet with schemes
of poetry sewed to educate the apron dawn.

Not exactly a hovel, not exactly a hearth;
"I think a taxi's like a little home," said
Marianne Moore,

this quilt's virago.

Clouet of Silks

Initially glimpsing
an ivory Pharoah figure
First Dynasty 3400

        quilted for warmth
        papyrus for words

stitchery sophisticated after *a.d.*
   tribesmanship
      later religious jaws went boning
after Renaissance windows, the straw
harshness strikes hangings rebut
      then
up went those quilts soft with their clout;
I'd like a little cloud here to nestle over the straw
I'd appreciate less straw more feathers
opposite types—straw and feathers—
like the moon nestling on thorns
      words you see through windows
threstled words tousled "La Lai del Desiré"
    Clouet of silks.

Medieval

Egotistical minutiae of *Stitch*

> Gambeson
> Habeton   MEDIEVAL
> Pourpoint
> Habergon

Worn simultaneously for protection
quilted medieval circuits

useless against fire
but charming and tender
as the wispy fingers
that stitched them

I like your hearth fire
it warms my fingers
skeins

weaving obsolete war garments.

From Water Mill

Only consider, said my author, contemporary painters
who bear a resemblance to quilts:

> Rauschenberg
> Johns
> Rivers

Reality could be their tassel
and Reality is there, that's what I think about a quilt
it's Reality, and it satisfied Rauschenberg.

Mushrooms on the village green
some white, some black,
some high, some short,
they gave a dimension to a pattern
weaving in and out in streams

that's Reality.

Once you start looking at real
mushrooms
you see art everywhere.

THE MUSHROOM QUILT FROM WATER MILL

Revered Quilts

Yesterday Andreas came here and I showed him my quilt
of Lord Byron in Albanian costume.
"Ah! His was an unnecessary loss," said Andreas.
"I don't think so, not nearly so much as the untimely
decease of Shelley. There was a real loss. And just
think of all the unfinished quilts—I mean—poems
he left. I consider them ideal losses." I couldn't

resist setting Andreas straight.
He then surprised me by mentioning the grave of Gramsci
in the Protestant Cemetery in Rome. "Gramsci was a
great loss," he whispered.
I then nearly shouted, "Only to the Quilt Party!
And you didn't even mention the grave of Keats in
that same cemetery. I consider him a supreme loss
to romantic quilts."
"Well we would have lost him anyway, considering
what century he was attempting to live in," said
Andreas. Kindly he added, "I too consider Keats cut
off in his prime, dropped like silk into calico scraps,
one of the losses of all time."

The Tooth Quilt

Say farewell o tooth like the Isle
of Lump no longer will you be connected
to the mainland.

Remember the Gandy Bridge going to St. Petersburg;
I remember canals and other indecent crossings over
the mud-struck crocodile river where the inlets
produced their flowers and the quiet, poisonous
links discourse with roots.

So shall you be severed. No stamp will be saved
in your name. No equipages gallop up to the post,
as in Guernsey when Hugo was in exile and Julie
lay under a quilt.

It will be silent as a residence for those
recovering from the Indian sun, or others in seek
of doctors. Remembering, as one says in the twilight,
the banyan quilt with its twisted ropes, recalled
the throat like the senior building, all
was struck, the Occident, the East, a brightness
nervous when the tongue left its theatre,
there where the first quilted words crept out:
"like dying the definite loss."

Marilyn Hacker

NEW YORK, NEW YORK

Feeling and Form

(for Sandy Moore & for Susanne K. Langer)

Dear San: Everybody doesn't write poetry.
A lot of people doodle profiles, write
something they think approximates poetry
because nobody taught them to read poetry.
Rhyming or trailing gerunds, clumps of words
straggle a page, unjustified—poetry?
It's not like talking, so it must be poetry.
Before they learn to write, all children draw
pictures grown-ups teach them how not to draw.
Anyone learns/ unlearns the craft of poetry
too. The fourth-grader who gets a neat like-
ness of Mom in crayon's not unlike

the woman who sent you her Tone Poem, who'd like
her admiration praised. That isn't poetry,
unless she did the work which makes it like
this, any, work, in outrage, love, or lik-

ing an apple's October texture. Write
about anything—I wish I could. It's like
the still-lives you love: you don't have to like
apples to like Cezanne. I do like words,
which is why I make things out of words
and listen to their hints, resounding like
skipping-stones radiating circles, draw-
ing context from text, the way I've watched you draw

a pepper-shaker on a table, draw
it again, once more, until it isn't like
anything but your idea of a draw-
ing, like an idea of movement, draw-
ing its shape from sequence. You write poetry.
I was a clever child who liked to draw,
and did it well, but when I watch you draw,
you rubber-face like I do when I write:
chewed lip, cat-tongue, smiles, scowls that go with right
choices, perplexed, deliberate, withdrawn
in worked play, conscious of the spaces words
or lines make as you make them, without words

for instant exegesis. Moulding words
around a shape's analogous to draw-
ing these coffee-cups in settings words
describe, but whose significance leaves words
unsaid, because it's drawn, because it's like
not my blue mug, but inked lines. Chosen words
—I couldn't write *your white mug*—collect words
they're meant, or drawn to, make mental space poetry
extends beyond the page. If you thought poetry
were merely nicely ordered private words
for two eyes only, why would you say, "Write
me a letter, dammit!" This is a letter, right?

Wrong. Form intimates fiction. I could write
me as a mathematician, weave in words
implying *you* a man, sixteen, a right-
handed abstract-expressionist. I'd write
untruths, from which some other *you* could draw
odd inferences. Though I don't, I write
you, and you're the Donor on the right-
hand panel, kneeling in sable kirtle. Like-
ly I'm the lady left of you, who'd like
to peer into your missal, where the writ-
ing (legible gothic) lauds in Latin poetry
the Lady at the center. Call her poetry,

virtual space, or Bona Dea. Poetry
dovetails contradictions. If I write
a private *you* a public discourse, words
tempered and stroked will draw you where you draw
these lines, and yours, convergent, made, unlike;

that likelihood draws words I write to poetry.

Contributors' Notes

JANE AUGUSTINE summers in the Colorado Rockies, the setting and metaphor for many poems in her book, *Lit by the Earth's Dark Blood* (Perishable Press). She has *The Women's Guide to Mountain Climbing* ready for publication. Her mixed media work, *U + I*, has been performed several times in the New York area. Twice a CAPS winner (1976, 1979), she teaches creative writing at Pratt Institute.

TOI DERRICOTTE works at Columbia University in a federal program to help school districts equalize opportunities in all areas of education. Poet-in-Residence for the New Jersey State Council on the Arts, she has completed over 50 residencies for them. Twice she won first prize in Academy of American Poets contests. Her poems appear in several anthologies and in her book, *Empress of the Death House* (Lotus, 1978).

SONYA DORMAN keeps a fine, organic garden on a cove of Connecticut's Mystic River. 1978–1980 were busy years for her in publishing. Her novel, *Planet Patrol* (Coward, McCann), an adventure story for girls, came out. In addition, her collection, *A Paper Raincoat* (Puckerbrush Press), was reprinted and a chapbook, *The Far Traveller* (Juniper), published.

KINERETH GENSLER teaches in the Radcliffe Seminars. She has translated work by the Israeli poet, Yehuda Amichai, as well as *Poems of Cyprus*. With Nina Nyhart she co-authored a textbook: *The Poetry Connection* (Teachers and Writers Collaborative of New York). Her Alice James Books collections are *Someone is Human*, which appears as one-third of *Threesome Poems*, and *Without Roof* (1981).

CELIA GILBERT was Poetry Editor of the Boston *Phoenix* from 1972–75. She co-authored and co-published *Women/Poems*, a magazine. In 1974 she won a Discovery Award from the 92nd Street YM-YWCA in New York. Her poetry has appeared in many magazines, including *The Paris Review* and *Poetry*. Viking printed her collected poems, *Queen of Darkness*, in 1977.

LOIS ELAINE GRIFFITH, who lives and works in Brooklyn, is both poet and playwright. *White Sirens* was produced at the New York Shakespeare Festival, and she is working on a new play, *Coconut Lounge*. Her first book of poetry is *Barbadian Fantasies*.

BARBARA GUEST lives on Long Island "with sky, sea, clouds, and great silences." She has published a novel, *Seeking Air* (Black Sparrow), as well as books of poems, among them: *Moscow Mansions* (Viking) and *The Countess from Minneapolis* (Burning Deck Press). Several years with *Art News* connected her and her work with many painters and their work.

AKUA LEZLI HOPE is a young, native New Yorker, black woman poet. She has been quoted as wanting "this journey sweet and each word undeniable." Her poems have appeared in *Hoodoo*, *Bopp*, *Essence*, and in anthologies. Her first original book is *Lovecycles* (Center for New Images, 1976). She makes money in marketing but takes time to seize images in photography and to study all the black musics.

BARBARA HOWES lives in Vermont. She and her son, Gregory Jay Smith, a sculptor, collaborated on an anthology, *The Sea-Green Horse*, when he was thirteen; recently he illustrated her book of short stories. Her awards span from a Guggenheim Fellowship in 1955 to the 1980 Bennington Award. Her sixth book of poems is *A Private Signal: Poems New & Selected* (1977). A chapbook is forthcoming.

COLLETTE INEZ was born in Brussels. She has received fellowships from the NEA and the New York CAPS program. Her poems are widely anthologized and appear in many magazines. Two published books are *The Woman Who Loved Worms* (Doubleday), which won a 1972 award, and *Alive and Taking Names* (Ohio University Press, 1977). "Light Takes Eight" is under consideration.

PHYLLIS JANOWITZ teaches in the writing program at Cornell. In 1979–80 she was an Alfred Hodder Fellow in the Humanities at Princeton. She has written four poetry books; *Rites of Strangers* (University Press of Virginia, 1978) was chosen by Elizabeth Bishop as winner of the Associated Writing Program Competition; her most recent book is *Visiting Rights*.

IRENA KLEPFISZ was born in Warsaw. She is founder and editor of *Conditions* magazine, for which she won an editorial fellowship in 1980 from the Coordinating Council of Literary Magazines. Some of her fiction and criticism, as well as a collection of poems, *Periods of Stress* (Piecework Press), have been published.

JOAN LARKIN lives with her teen-age daughter in Brooklyn, where she has organized and taught numerous women's writing workshops. She is co-editor (and a contributor) of the forthcoming *Lesbian Poetry: An Anthology* (Persephone Press) as well as co-editor of *Amazon Poetry*. (For additional information see the end note to our interview of Audre Lorde by Joan Larkin.)

ANN LAUTERBACH spent several years in London, where she edited art books and taught at St. Martin's School of Art. There she conducted a seminar investigating possible correlatives between decision-making situations in art and life. Her poetry includes *Many Times, but Then* (University of Texas Press, 1979) and *Later That Evening* (Bevan Davies, 1981).

KATHLEEN LIGNELL now lives on the mid-coast of Maine. She received *Carolina Quarterly*'s 1978 poetry award and has published a chapbook, *The Calamity Jane Poems* (Rosebud Press, 1979; reprinted by *A Press*, 1980). In the seventies she was program coordinator in literature at the University of California Extension, Berkeley. Formerly a correspondent for the *Bangor Daily News*, she now teaches at the Penobscot Consortium.

CYNTHIA MACDONALD is a winner of many awards for poetry, including a 1976 CAPS grant. She has received grants from the NEA for both her poetry and her music. Her libretto, *The Rehearsal*, was performed at three university and opera festivals. Both her poetry and her essays have been widely published and anthologized; additionally, she reviews work of women writers for *The Washington Post*. (For information about her books, see the end note to our essay on Marie Ponsot by Cynthia Macdonald.)

JUDITH MCDANIEL lives in very rural upstate New York. Since 1975, she's taught at Skidmore College, where she has assumed many administrative duties to help further the arts and women's opportunities. Recently she was a CAPS Fellow in fiction. With Maureen Brady, she has founded a new feminist publishing company, Spinsters, Ink. Spinsters published her *Reconstituting the World: The Poetry and Vision of Adrienne Rich* (1979).

KRISTINA MCGRATH has worked for the New York State Poets-in-the-Schools program for six years. In addition, she has conducted adult writing workshops. She was a CAPS fellow, 1977. *Voices for Two Women Who Speak and Dance*, a dance theater piece, has been produced in New York City and Chicago. Recently, she completed a novel. Her poetry credits include such publications as *Harper's* and *The Paris Review*.

SARA MILES has been a translator and teacher, besides being an editor and writer. Her poetry has appeared in *Essence* and *Ms.*, as well as in anthologies, and her essays, reviews, and criticism have been in such publications as *The Washington Post*, *The London Times*, *The Feminist Review*. Recently she was chosen to receive an NEA 1981–82 Fellowship for Creative Writers. (For additional information see the end note to our essay on June Jordan by Sara Miles.)

JANE MILLER holds an M.F.A. from Iowa. On the permanent faculty of Goddard College, she teaches poetry and literature. She worked in radio production of Feminist Program for Berkeley's KPFA and holds a Class III broadcasting license. She has also been a sculptor's assistant. *Many Junipers, Heartbeats* is recently out from Copper Beech Press.

JUDITH MOFFETT teaches English at the University of Pennsylvania, where she took her doctorate. This is her third year as a staff assistant at Bread Loaf. One of her books, *Gentleman, Single, Refined and Selected Poems 1937–1959* by Hjalmar Gullberg (LSU Press), translations from the Swedish, won a Columbia Translation Prize in 1978. *Keeping Time* (1976) also was published by LSU.

HONOR MOORE moves from poetry writing to play writing to writing about poetry and plays to teaching the writing of plays and poetry. She was awarded a 1975 CAPS grant in playwriting. For 1981–82 she received an NEA grant. Her books are *Leaving and Coming Back* (Effie's Press) and the more recently completed collection of poems *The You That Lives On in Me*.

ROBIN MORGAN's publisher is Random House. Her two books of poems are *Monster* and *Lady of the Beasts* (1972, 1976). And her latest prose is *Going Too Far: The Personal Chronicle of a Feminist* (forthcoming, 1982). She is working on a cycle of verse plays. A children's novel, *The Mer-Child: A New Legend*, is also forthcoming.

CAROL MUSKE teaches in the M.F.A. Writing Program of Columbia University and directs a writing program for women in prison called Art without Walls. She serves on P.E.N.'s Freedom-to-Write and Prison Writing Committees. Her poems have appeared in many anthologies and magazines and her own two books, the most recent: *Skylight* (Doubleday, 1981).

SHARON OLDS lives in New York and is Lecturer-in-Residence on poetry at the Theodor Herzl Institute. Of her received grants, the most recent (1981–82) is from the NEA. *Satan Says* (University of Pittsburgh Press, 1980) was published in the Pitt Poetry Series. Her poems are published in many magazines and she does frequent readings in the New York area.

MARGE PIERCY has been particularly active in causes serving women. The list of her poetry readings and writing workshops covers the continent. Among many other honors, she received the Literature Award from the Massachusetts Governor's Commission on the Status of Women. Her three recent (of seven) poetry books were published by Knopf—the latest, *The Moon Is Always Female*. Her new novel is *Vida* (Summit, 1980).

NTOZAKE SHANGE, a 1981–82 NEA grant recipient, has been a visiting lecturer at New York University, Yale and Brown, among others. The first of her eight theatrical credits was *for colored girls who have considered suicide/when the rainbow is enuf.* Her collected plays, *3 Pieces: Spell # 7, Boogie Woogie Landscapes, and A Photograph* were published in 1981 by St. Martin's Press.

JUDITH JOHNSON SHERWIN is the author of eight books, seven poetry and one fiction. *Uranium Poems* (1969) won the Yale Younger Poets Prize and was re-printed in 1981 by AMS Press. Two other books are *The Life Riot* and *Impossible Buildings.* She is a consultant for Poets and Writers, Inc., and is active in The Poetry Society of America. She is also a 1981–82 NEA grantee.

KATHLEEN SPIVACK has published poetry and prose in many magazines and anthologies. The most recent of her three books is *Swimmer in the Spreading Dawn* (Applewood Press, 1981). She has received several grants, including one from the NEA and another from the Massachusetts Artists Foundation. At present, she directs an advanced writing workshop at Cambridge, Massachusetts.

CELIA WATSON STROME has had poems in such publications as *New River, Forum, The Smith.* She has also received five awards for poetry, including the John Crowe Ransom Prize. She taught as Poet-in-Residence in the Greenwich (Connecticut) elementary and junior high schools, in a program she had initiated. The poems appearing in this anthology are from her book manuscript "The Voices."

ELLEN WITTLINGER has published *Breakers* (Sheep Meadow Press, 1979). She also writes plays; two of these, *Close to Home* and *Cabbages,* have been presented in staged readings in Boston. She was a fellow for two years at the Fine Arts Work Center in Provincetown, Massachusetts. Her poems have appeared in many magazines and in anthologies.

YVONNE is the poetry editor of *Ms.* She also teaches writing at Hunter College and New York University. A narrative poet, she is working on a three volume epic poem about a family of black native American women. Excerpts of this work have appeared in many magazines and anthologies, most recently in *The Third Woman* (Houghton Mifflin, 1980).

Gift Orders

Please enter a ☐ 1 volume   ☐ 2 volume
☐ 4 volume (complete set) gift order sent to:

Recipient _____

Address _____

_____

City _____

State _____   Zip _____

Recipient _____

Address _____

_____

City _____

State _____   Zip _____

Recipient _____

Address _____

_____

City _____

State _____   Zip _____

A Gift
to you for

from

Woman Poet
P.O. Box 12668
Reno, Nevada
89510

Gift Book Subscriptions

Recipients will receive the below (left) gift an-
nouncement signed by you; gift orders begin with
the first volume in the series (*The West*), unless
requested otherwise.

Collectors' Copies: Hard Cover Limited Editions:
$12.95 plus $1.00 handling.
Soft Cover Regular Editions: Individuals $6.00
each plus $1.00 handling, Institutions $9.00 each.

Two volume orders, for example, *The West* and
The East: Soft Cover—Individuals $11.00,
Students $10.00, Institutions $16.00. Hard
Cover—$23.00.
(*Countries other than U.S. add $2.00 postage.*)

Set of four regional volumes, beginning with the
inaugural volume unless requested otherwise: Soft
Cover—Individuals $20.00, Students $18.00,
Institutions $28.00. Hard Cover—$45.00.
(*Countries other than U.S. add $3.00 postage.*)

Please enter my order for myself.

I want _____.

Total enclosed: $ _____ Date: _____

Name _____

Address _____

_____

City _____ State _____ Zip _____

Mail with your check or purchase order to
Woman Poet, Women-in-Literature, Incorporated,
P.O. Box 12668, Reno, Nevada, 89510.